# Privacy in Employment Law

## 1996 Supplement

# Privacy in Employment Law

## 1996 Supplement

Matthew W. Finkin

*Professor of Law*
*University of Illinois College of Law*

BNA BOOKS

The Bureau of National Affairs, Inc., Washington, D.C.

**Library of Congress Cataloging-in-Publication Data**

Finkin, Matthew W.
Privacy in employment law / Matthew W. Finkin
p. cm.
Includes index.
ISBN 0-87179-883-2
1. Personnel records--law and legislation--United States.
2. Confidential communications--Personnel records--United States.
3. Privacy, Right of--United States. I. Title.
KF3457.5.F56 1995
344.73'0125--dc20
[347.304125]

94-49404
CIP



Published by BNA Books
1250 23rd St. NW, Washington, DC 20037
International Standard Book Number: 0-57018-037-7
*Printed in the United States of America*

# DETAILED TABLE OF CONTENTS

# BNA BOOKS CUSTOMER SATISFACTION SURVEY

BNA Books, *A Division of* The Bureau of National Affairs, Inc.

8. Is there any area in which you think we can improve?

_____ Customer Service _____ Editorial Content _____ Quality

_____ Timeliness _____ Other (explain):

_______________________________________________

_______________________________________________

_______________________________________________

Would you like us to contact you? ____ Yes ____ No

Name:______________________ Phone #:______________

Additional Comments: _______________________________

_______________________________________________

_______________________________________________

_______________________________________________

*Fold here and seal*

- - - - - - - - - - - - - - - - - - - - - - - - - - - - - - - - -

NO POSTAGE
NECESSARY
IF MAILED
IN THE
UNITED STATES

**BUSINESS REPLY MAIL**

First Class Permit No. 10089 Washington, D.C.

***POSTAGE WILL BE PAID BY ADDRESSEE—***

THE BUREAU OF NATIONAL AFFAIRS INC
BNA BOOKS
ATTN M S PIRTHIPAL
1250 23RD STREET NW
WASHINGTON DC 20077-6742

**PART II—STATUTORY AND REGULATORY REFERENCES**

## PART III—SAMPLE BUSINESS FORMS[1]



[1]Forms are reprinted from *BNA's Policy and Practice Series.* They are designed to be used as "starting points" for the discussion and/or creation of a policy or procedure, and may be adapted to particular work environments. Users should be aware that the samples are illustrative only. Employers always should check with their legal counsel and review federal, state, and local laws or regulations (as well as conditions and terms of union contracts, if appropriate) before fashioning and putting into effect any guidance or procedure modeled after any of the samples contained herein. Many of these forms, and others, are available on disk in *BNA's Personnel Policy Writer* from BNA Plus, 1-800-452-7773.

# INTRODUCTION

The final report of the Privacy Protection Study Commission, issued in 1977, issued a set of recommendations for voluntary adoption by private employers governing fair information practices—limiting the nature of information to be collected, informing employees of their information practices, limiting disclosure, providing for employee access and correction, and providing for periodic review to assure compliance.[1] Employee survey data conducted by Louis Harris & Associates in 1993 indicated a high level of employee confidence in employer data collection practices.[2] But, the repose of confidence predicated upon these data has been placed in question by a survey of 84 responding Fortune 500 companies, representing 3.2 million employees, directed by Professor David Linowes, who had served as chairman of the Privacy Protection Study Commission.[3] Among the more salient findings are:

- nearly half the corporations collect information on employees without informing the individual concerned.
- most corporations give employees access to personal office records, although nearly three-quarters do not give access to supervisors' records.
- about half of the companies do not conduct systematic evaluation of their record-keeping practices with an eye toward confidentiality safeguards.

The study concluded among other things that:

> Often information of a personal nature is collected and included along with pertinent personnel data. Employees may not be aware of the types of data collected, methods of collection, or the sources consulted. Even medical information and sometimes the results of drug testing are included. Employees are,

---

[1]Report of the Privacy Protection Study Commission, PERSONAL PRIVACY IN AN INFORMATION SOCIETY Ch. 6 (1977).

[2]Louis Harris & Associates, WORKPLACE HEALTH AND PRIVACY ISSUES (1994). These data are usefully supplemented by another rigorous study, Albert Cantril and Susan Cantril, LIVE AND LET LIVE: AMERICAN PUBLIC OPINION ABOUT PRIVACY AT HOME AND AT WORK (1994).

[3]David Linowes, A Research Survey of Privacy in the Workplace (April, 1996).

> in many instances, denied access to all or portions of their own files while the employer may release the same information to third parties. Employees who are allowed access to files may not be allowed to correct errors in the information.[4]

The principal investigator called for legislation to provide the necessary safeguards.

In sum, a substantial engagement with questions of employee privacy has been called for. Suffice it to say, any such general reflection on the content of the American law of worker privacy—by the legislatures, the courts, the bar, and academics—might draw upon the law in other industrialized democracies.[5]

---

[4] *Id.* at 28.

[5] *See e.g.*, *Worker Privacy*, *17* COMP. LAB. L.J. 1-205 (1995) (a ten nation study); and *Privacy in the Workplace: International Perspectives* in Proceedings of the Forty-Eighth Annual Meeting of the National Academy of Arbitrators Ch. 7 (Joyce Najita ed. 1996).

# Part I

# An Analysis of Privacy in the Employment Relationship

CHAPTER 1

# MEDICAL SCREENING AND TESTING

## I. BASES OF MEDICAL SCREENING

### C. Constitutional Constraints

Where a public mass transit authority adopted a fitness program for its police officers that included a pregnancy (urine) test, the question was presented of whether such a requirement met constitutional standards.[1] The suit withstood the employer's motion for summary judgment. Although the plaintiff characterized her claim as deriving from a right to privacy, Judge Pollak saw it as grounded in the Fourth Amendment's protection against unreasonable search and seizure. The court noted that what is required under the Fourth Amendment is a comparison of the employees' privacy interest with the employer's interest in conducting the test. The court characterized the former as "very strong" insofar as it related to informational self-determination:

> In addition to their direct interest in maintaining their privacy as to the fact of their pregnancy, SEPTA's employees might have a wide range of other reasons to wish to avoid a pregnancy test. These could include fear of disclosure to fellow employees; the desire to avoid disclosing a subsequent miscarriage or abortion; and the desire to avoid possible stigma or discrimination by their employer. The reasonable expectations of privacy of a police officer may be somewhat diminished because of intrusions on privacy ordinarily associated with her profession.[2]

However, there was no evidence at this stage of whether the officer's work circumstances had diminished her expectation of privacy. Turning, then, to the employer's interest, the court found the argument "close" to demonstrating the requisite showing of "compelling interest," but held that the employer had failed to show the impracticality of designing a fitness program that posed a minimal risk to pregnant employees.[3]

---

[1]Ascolese v. Southeastern Pa. Transp. Auth., 902 F. Supp. 533 (E.D. Pa. 1995).

[2]*Id.* at 550 (citing Vernonia School Dist. 47J v. Acton, 115 S. Ct. 2386, 2392–93 (1995) (stating that, inter alia, the "communal undress" of locker rooms and the physical examinations associated with student participation in athletics reduce student athletes' reasonable expectations of privacy)).

[3]*Id.*

The court also held it premature to grant the employer's motion for summary judgment on the issue of whether a warrant was required for the employee to submit to the test: such a requirement would have ensured employees of advance notice of the test and its officially sanctioned character; there was no need to administer the test unexpectedly or quickly; nor would the securing of a warrant be especially burdensome.

## II. GENETIC SCREENING AND MONITORING

### B. State Statutory Regulation of Genetic Testing

New Hampshire now forbids genetic testing as a condition of employment, in contrast to genetic monitoring which is permitted upon written and informed consent.[4] The relevant provision reads:

> *Use of Genetic Testing in Employment Situations*
>
> I. No employer, labor organization, employment agency, or licensing agency shall directly or indirectly:
>
> (a) Solicit, require or administer genetic testing relating to any individual as a condition of employment, labor organization membership, or licensure.
>
> (b) Affect the terms, conditions, or privileges of employment, labor organization membership, or licensure or terminate the employment, labor organization membership, or licensure of any individual based on genetic testing.
>
> II. Except as provided in paragraph IV of this section, no person shall sell or otherwise provide to an employer, labor organization, employment agency or licensing agency any genetic testing relating to an employee, labor organization member or licensee or to a prospective employee, labor organization member or licensee.
>
> III. Any agreement between an employer, labor organization, employment agency, or licensing agency and an individual offering employment, labor organization membership, licensure, or any pay or benefit to that individual in return for taking a genetic test is prohibited.
>
> IV. This section shall not prohibit the genetic testing of an employee who requests to undergo genetic testing and who provides written and informed consent to genetic testing for any of the following purposes:
>
> (a) Investigating a worker's compensation claim . . .
>
> (b) Determining the employee's susceptibility or level of exposure to potentially toxic chemicals or potentially toxic substances in the workplace, if the employer does not terminate the employee, or take any other action that adversely affects any term, condition, or privilege of the employee's employment, as a result of genetic testing.

---

[4]N.H. REV. STATS., Ch. 141-H (1995 Cum. Supp.).

> V. This section shall not prohibit or limit genetic testing for evidence of insurability with respect to life, disability income, or long-term care insurance under the terms of an employee benefit plan.[5]

A "genetic test" is defined as:

> a test, examination, or analysis which is generally accepted in the scientific and medical communities for the purpose of identifying the presence, absence, or alteration of any gene or chromosome, and any report, interpretation, or evaluation of such a test, examination, or analysis, but excludes any otherwise lawful test, examination, or analysis that is undertaken for the purpose of determining whether an individual meets reasonable functional standards for a specific job or task.[6]

## III. DISCLOSURE OF AND ACCESS TO MEDICAL RECORDS AND REPORTS

### C. Employee Access to Medical Records Under State Law

#### *1. Psychological Tests*

In *Cleghorn v. Hess,*[7] a guard employed by a security contractor at a nuclear weapons facility submitted to a psychological evaluation, as federal regulations required. When he later sought a copy of his psychological records and tests results pursuant to state law requiring the disclosure of health care records to patients, his request was denied. The Supreme Court of Nevada held that the records had to be supplied: an employee subject to a psychological evaluation was a statutory "patient"—the lack of a physician–patient relationship (for malpractice purposes) and the lack of a therapeutic purpose notwithstanding—and requiring the disclosure was in keeping with the purpose of the statute:

> Wackenhut employees are examined, tested, and evaluated by Dr. Hess, a licenced psychologist, to determine if they are "psychologically suitable" for employment. Yet, after being subjected to this examination, the employees themselves are then denied access to the results of that testing. Adverse information in the employees' personnel files could, unbeknownst to the employees, materially affect their future, without the employees having had an opportunity to challenge the purported results. . . . Denying employees access to their own files allows employers to gather secret information on their employees with impunity.[8]

---

[5] *Id.*, Ch. 141-H:3.

[6] *Id.*, Ch. 141-H:1(IV). [As this supplement went to press, the New Jersey legislature passed a prohibition on genetic screening that is awaiting the governor's disposition.]

[7] 853 P.2d 1260, 8 IER Cases 1047 (Nev. 1993).

[8] *Id.* at 1263.

The court was also unpersuaded by the fact that the evaluation was required by federal regulations:

> It is as if to say we can trust "Big Brother" to look after our best interest. We have found from experience that government functions best when subject to reasonable scrutiny. Information should be withheld from citizens who are affected by it only when truly merited, such as when a national security reason is established. Showing an employee his or her psychological test result surely will not compromise national security.[9]

## D. State Statutory Restrictions on Disclosure of Medical Records and Reports

In *Edwards v. Board of Trustees of the State Employees Group Benefits Program*,[10] the Inspector General of Louisiana petitioned for access to the medical records of the state employees' group benefits carrier in an investigation of fraud and waste. The Louisiana Court of Appeals held the investigative purpose outweighed the individuals' privacy interest, but it stressed the carefully crafted nature of the inquiry as limited to claim records only, not medical information:

> [T]he limited disclosure, as requested in plaintiffs' petition, of only "those claims that are the subject of this examination *with all medical information (i.e., information concerning diagnosis, prognosis, treatment, etc.) covered and concealed* in a way that allows inspection, examination and copying of the original documents without revealing medical information" does not constitute an invasion of a right of privacy protected by the state or federal constitution.[11]

## E. Common Law Limits on Disclosure of Medical Records and Reports

### *2. Privacy*

The application of the common law of privacy to the disclosure of medical reports in general—and of being HIV positive in particular—was considered by the Colorado Court of Appeals in *Borquez v. Ozer.*[12] Borquez was a lawyer in the Ozer firm. Immediately upon learning that his companion had been diagnosed with AIDS, and being advised by his physician to be tested immediately, he felt unable to represent a client that day and, in discussion with a partner in the firm in an effort to locate a replacement, he disclosed his homosexuality, his relationship, and his

---

[9]*Id.*
[10]644 So. 2d 776 (La. Ct. App. 1994).
[11]*Id.* at 778.
[12]11 IER Cases 496 (Colo. App. 1995).

need for AIDS testing, requesting that this information be kept confidential. The partner made no express commitment to confidentiality, and within days these facts became common knowledge among the employees and shareholders of the firm.

The Court of Appeals sustained the jury verdict for the plaintiff on invasion of privacy grounds. It held, reviewing authority on point, that the disclosure was of a "private" matter (i.e., "would be highly objectionable to a reasonable person because a strong stigma still attaches to both homosexuality and AIDS"). Second and, perhaps, more important, it held the scope of disclosure ("publication") has to be measured by the sensitive nature of the information and the relationship of the parties:

> Communication to the general public has not been required by some courts because disclosure to those persons with whom the plaintiff has a special relationship may be just as devastating as disclosure to many. . . .
>
> An invasion of a plaintiff's right to privacy is important if it exposes private facts to a public whose knowledge of those facts would be embarrassing to the plaintiff. . . . Accordingly, we hold that it is appropriate to recognize the tort of invasion of privacy in the form of unreasonable publicity given to the private life of another in the circumstances of this case where private information was unreasonably disseminated to fellow employees who had no legitimate interest therein.[13]

The court concluded that Borquez's coworkers—lawyers and support staff—were a "public" with whom he had a special relationship and to whom the disclosure would prove particularly embarrassing. It also rejected the firm's arguments to waiver or consent, and to qualified privilege—on the latter point holding that a qualified privilege for the shareholders of the firm to discuss Borquez's condition among themselves was exceeded by the broader communication.

The privilege of a psychiatrist and a psychologist to disclose the homicidal tendency of a patient to the police and the intended target (a federal judge) respectively was affirmed in *In re Viviano.*[14] In view of the trial court's failure to charge the jury on the underlying invasion of privacy claim, the appellate court undertook to consider the facts de novo. Although the expert testimony was conflicting, the court credited the fact that one of the therapists had consulted an attorney (who represented the state medical society and who advised him that he had a duty to warn of threats), the deadly seriousness of the threats, and the fact that involuntary commitment would not necessarily have obviated the threat inasmuch as such patients have been released without notice. It found that the disclosure, balanced against the patient's privacy interest, was reasonable.

[13]*Id.* at 502 (quoting Beaumont v. Brown 257 N.W.2d 522 (1977)).

[14]645 So. 2d 1301 (La. Ct. App. 1994).

In *Doe v. Methodist Hospital,*[15] a hospital employee told her husband—a coworker of the patient—that the coworker had tested positive for HIV. The hospital's motion for summary judgment on the patient's suit for invasion of privacy was denied (and not appealed).

New York does not recognize a common law right to privacy. It has a statutory right limited to commercial appropriation of one's name or portrait, which has been taken to preclude any more extensive common law development. In *Waldron v. Ball Corp.,*[16] an employee had died of a rare form of leukemia. A second employee contracted the same disease and filed a workers' compensation claim. The employer sought permission of the administrator of the decedent's estate (her husband) for access to her medical records to assist the company in preparing the workers' compensation case; the husband refused, citing the personal nature of the records and his desire to "put everything behind him." The company then wrongfully used a medical expense reimbursement form signed by the husband to secure the medical records from the decedent's hospital. The Appellate Division sustained the grant for summary judgment for the company on theories of invasion of privacy and emotional distress. On the former, it found there to be no cause of action by operation of the statute and the construction given it. The court agreed that New York acknowledged the confidentiality of information acquired during medical treatment, but concluded that no private cause of action is created to vindicate that confidentiality in this setting. (Thus it avoided reaching the question of whether or not such a breach survived the death of the patient.) Neither did it find an adequate ground in the spouse's emotional distress: without condoning the methods used to obtain the records, the court held that the company had not exceeded all bounds of decency.

## F. Constitutional Restriction of Disclosure

The constitutional status of the disclosure of medical records was considered by the U.S. Court of Appeals for the Third Circuit in *Doe v. Southeastern Pennsylvania Transportation Authority (SEPTA).*[17] As part of a cost containment and review program for SEPTA's health care program, the chief administrative officer requested reports from the pharmacy authorized to be the sole dispenser of drugs prescribed for SEPTA employees under its self-insurance program. These reports covered employees filling prescriptions of $100 or more per month and included, inter alia, the name of the prescribing doctor, the name of the drug, the

---

[15]639 N.E.2d 683 (Ind. Ct. App. 1994).
[16]619 N.Y.S.2d 841, 11 IER Cases 417 (App. Div. 1994).
[17]72 F.3d 1133 (3d Cir. 1995).

number of days supplied and, most important here, the name of the employee. The prescriptions listed for the plaintiff were on the list, and upon inquiry to SEPTA's staff physician and chief physician, the administrator learned that the drugs prescribed for the plaintiff were used exclusively for HIV or AIDS-related conditions. The staff physician informed the patient of the administrator's inquiries, and the patient sued and prevailed at trial under the Civil Rights Act. The Third Circuit reversed.

Judge Rosenn held as a constitutional matter that individuals have a "limited right to privacy in their medical records," stating that

> [i]t is now possible from looking at an individual's prescription records to determine that person's illnesses, or even to ascertain such private facts as whether a woman is attempting to conceive a child through the use of fertility drugs. This information is precisely the sort intended to be protected by penumbras of privacy. . . . An individual using prescription drugs has a right to expect that such information will customarily remain private.[18]

Because the information needed by the SEPTA administrator could have been coded without using the names of the particular employees (as it later was), the employee/patient's right of privacy was implicated. But, the court stressed, SEPTA had not requested the employee/patient's names as part of the information it sought; thus the disclosure was inadvertently received.

Moreover, the court thought the extent of disclosure "too thin" to support an invasion of privacy claim; that is, only the administrator and her subordinate, SEPTA's director of benefits, learned the plaintiff's name from the report.[19] The medical staff consulted were already aware of the plaintiff's condition. Thus the extent of disclosure had to be weighed against the legitimate public purpose served by the disclosure, and these factors weighed in favor of the government (i.e., its need to protect against fraud and abuse of its prescription drug insurance). The court stressed the inadvertent nature of the disclosure, its limited scope, the fact that the employee suffered no adverse job-related actions by the employer, and that the possibility of future disclosure was swiftly rectified. But Judge Rosenn noted as well that there may be occasions when the disclosure of the names of individual patients would be justified.[20] Judge Lewis dis-

---

[18] *Id.* at 1138.

[19] *Id.* at 1139.

[20] *Id.* at 1142 n.5:

> There may be situations not before us now where an employer who pays for prescriptions or benefits for employees or their dependents may need to know the identity of a person obtaining the prescriptions or benefits. After all, an employer might need this information to determine whether the person obtaining the prescriptions or benefits was eligible for them, or if the person was even an employee. Of course, such need to know would have to comply with the employee's right of privacy as well.

sented in part on the ground that the court's approach would make it "far easier in the future for employers to disclose their employees' private medical information, obtained during an audit of the company's health benefits plan."[21]

## G. Federal Statutory Restriction of Disclosure

The federal Drug Abuse Office and Treatment Act of 1972, as amended in 1992, provides in pertinent part:

> Records of the identity, diagnosis, prognosis, or treatment of any patient which are maintained in connection with the performance of any program or activity relating to substance abuse education, prevention, training, treatment, rehabilitation, or research, which is conducted, regulated, or directly or indirectly assisted by any department or agency of the United States shall, except as provided in subsection (e) of this section, be confidential and be disclosed only for the purposes and under the circumstances expressly authorized under subsection (b) of this section.[22]

Given the breadth of federal assistance—direct or indirect—in drug treatment and rehabilitation, the provision has potentially a very broad sweep. Provision is made for disclosure upon the patient's written consent in certain circumstances. But the U.S. Court of Appeals for the Sixth Circuit has held that a private right of action cannot be implied under the Act.[23]

---

[21]*Id.* at 1147 (Lewis, C.J., concurring and dissenting).
[22]42 U.S.C. §290dd-2 (1995).
[23]Ellison v. Cocke County, Tenn., 63 F.3d 467, 10 IER Cases 1658 (6th Cir. 1995).

CHAPTER 2

# DRUG, ALCOHOL, AND TOBACCO SCREENING AND TESTING

## III. THE LAW OF DRUG TESTING

### A. Federal Regulation

#### *1. Constitutional Constraints*

In *Chandler v. Miller,*[1] the Eleventh Circuit confronted a Georgia statute requiring a medical certification of the absence of five drugs as a condition of candidacy for certain elective public offices. The law was challenged on Fourth Amendment, equal protection, and First Amendment grounds and survived scrutiny under each. Apropos the first, the majority stressed the discretion given the states to determine qualifications for public office and the rational relationship between qualification and the end sought:

> [T]hose vested with the highest executive authority to make public policy in general and frequently to supervise Georgia's drug interdiction efforts in particular must be persons appreciative of the perils of drug use.
>
> But drug use poses significant dangers beyond rendering elected officials unsympathetic to drug interdiction efforts. The nature of high public office in itself demands the highest levels of honesty, clear-sightedness, and clear-thinking.[2]

Nor, in the court's opinion, did the law infringe on freedom of expression.

Judge Barkett dissented, stating that the question was not the incompatibility of drug use with high elective office, but whether a warrantless search is constitutionally permissible

> when there is no individualized suspicion, when there is no immediate or direct threat to public safety, when those being searched are not directly involved in the frontlines of drug interdiction, when there is no institutional setting involved such as a prison or public school requiring swift and informal discipline, and when there are no dire consequences as a result of waiting to obtain a warrant if a candidate, or anyone else for that matter, is suspected of violating

[1]73 F.3d 1543 (11th Cir. 1996).

[2]*Id.* at 1546.

> the law. The first question for the court is *not* whether the state's interest is great enough and its chosen method effective enough to outweigh the privacy interests involved.[3]

Thus he saw no *special* governmental need served by the law as required by the U.S. Supreme Court's gloss on point:

> I recognize that employment choices may indeed diminish expectations of privacy. An individual need not choose to become a drug interdiction agent, military intelligence officer, or railway engineer, thereby avoiding the intensive training and intrusive screening required by that particular job. But, an individual does not have a constitutional right to a specific kind of employment. The Constitution, however, protects participation in government. While candidates relinquish to the people a great deal of their privacy in choosing to run for public office, the price should not include sacrificing one's Fourth Amendment right to be free from unreasonable searches and seizures.[4]

Barkett also found the First Amendment implications more persuasive than did the majority.[5]

Where a union of publicly employed firefighters had agreed with the employing city to the conduct of random drug testing, but did not agree on the precise procedure to be used, a federal district court held a procedure that required "direct supervision"—that is, observation of the employee while the sample was given (but not including observation of the donor's genitals)—not to be constitutionally unreasonable.[6] The use of a monitor was held to provide better security than that afforded by the prior policy of specimen donation in a "dry room":

> The Court finds persuasive the testimony of Defendants' expert, Dr. Clossen, who testified that use of a dry room enables an employee to avoid detection in a variety of ways. Most obvious, Dr. Clossen testified that an employee

---

[3]*Id.* at 1550 (Barkett, J., dissenting).

[4]*Id.* at 1552.

[5]The majority maintains that the government's purpose is not suppression of free expression. Yet, it supports its holding by citing the importance of ensuring that elected officials are "persons appreciative of the perils of drug use" and "[]sympathetic to drug interdiction efforts." Establishing a certain ideology as a "qualification" for holding public office appears to be a content-based restriction on free expression. Drug policy is a politically charged issue confronting many government officials who have disparate points of view regarding the "Drug War" and the efficacy of the means employed in fighting it. It is the function of public office holders to write, enforce, and interpret the laws, including drug laws. By conditioning holding public office upon submission to drug screening, however, the Georgia legislature effectively bans from positions of political power not only those candidates who might disagree with the current policy criminalizing drug use, but also those who challenge the intrusive governmental means to detect such use among its citizenry. This statute is neither neutral nor procedural, but, in the majority's own characterization, attempts to ensure that only candidates with a certain point of view qualify for public office.

*Id.* (footnote omitted).

[6]Wilcher v. City of Wilmington, 891 F. Supp. 993 (D. Del. 1995).

> could carry clean urine into the dry room and substitute it for his own. The Court finds that use of a monitor virtually eliminates this and other types of sample tampering.
>
> On a human level, the Court is mindful of the possible embarrassment one may feel at having to urinate in the presence of another. The Court notes that excretory functions are highly personal and generally should be afforded maximum privacy. Nevertheless, the Court finds that a direct supervision method while invasive is not by its nature constitutionally unreasonable.[7]

The court buttressed its conclusion by pointing out that the U.S. Supreme Court in *Skinner v. Railway Labor Executives' Association*[8] had "noted the desirability of furnishing urine samples under the 'direct observation' of a monitor . . . to ensure the integrity of the sample."[9] But the full passage relied upon read:

> We recognize, however, that the procedures for collecting the necessary samples, which require employees to perform an excretory function traditionally shielded by great privacy, raise concerns not implicated by blood or breath tests. While we would not characterize these additional privacy concerns as minimal in most contexts, we note that the regulations endeavor to reduce the intrusiveness of the collection process. The regulations do *not* require that samples be furnished under the direct observation of a monitor, *despite* the desirability of such a procedure to ensure the integrity of the sample.[10]

It would seem that the Supreme Court had stressed the less-intrusive character of the procedure as weighing in support of its constitutionality; if so, it remains to be seen whether the conclusion drawn by the district court has turned the Court's opinion on its head.

In *Dykes v. Southeastern Pennsylvania Transportation Authority,*[11] the Third Circuit confronted the application of a policy allowing the testing of a bus driver upon "reasonable suspicion" of drug use.[12] The parties conceded this standard to be permissible under the Fourth Amendment. The employee challenged that reasonable cause was not evidenced, an issue that could have been raised through the grievance arbitration clause of an applicable collective bargaining agreement, but that was not pursued to arbitration. The court held that whether or not there was "reasonable suspicion" to require a drug and alcohol test had to be decided via the grievance arbitration procedure. It noted, in keeping with authority elsewhere, that such a hearing would provide such due process as would meet constitutional muster. But the court went a good deal further, relying on Third Circuit precedent (concerning the scope of an exclusive bargain-

---

[7]*Id.* at 1001 (footnote omitted).
[8]489 U.S. 602, 4 IER Cases 224 (1989).
[9]Wilcher v. City of Wilmington, 891 F. Supp. at 1002 n.3. (D. Del. 1995).
[10]Skinner v. Railway Labor Executives' Ass'n, 489 U.S. at 626 (1989) (emphasis added).
[11]68 F.3d 1564 (3d Cir. 1995), *petition for cert. filed* (U.S. Feb. 7, 1996) (No. 95-7810).
[12]*Id.* at 1570.

ing agreement's authority to make contracts and settlements binding on members of the bargaining unit) as establishing "that even where a drug testing policy has been held to be constitutionally infirm, a public employee may not pursue a civil rights suit based upon that infirmity where his union and his employer agree to operate under that policy."[13]

The theory, in other words, is one of consent (or waiver) implied in law; that is, inasmuch as the individual could consent to an unconstitutional condition—or, perhaps more accurately, to waive the unconstitutional condition—a union clothed with authority to negotiate terms and conditions of employment that bind all members of the unit it represents could consent to (or waive) for each individual unit member it represents the very same otherwise unconstitutional condition. The union's authority derives as a matter of law (i.e., because a majority of the members of the bargaining unit designated or selected it, the union becomes the exclusive bargaining representative for all, irrespective of a dissenting unit member's personal desires). Consequently, the theory has been criticized on that very ground:

> [T]he transference of the power to waive due process from the individual to a collective cannot be reconciled with the Constitution. The fourteenth amendment, like the first amendment, is a limit upon government. "A citizen's constitutional rights can hardly be infringed simply because a majority of the people choose that it be." It follows that one's right to due process cannot be infringed simply because a majority of one's fellow workers choose that it be. The waiver theory would improperly foreclose scrutiny of whether a governmental employer has acted in contravention of the limits imposed by the fourteenth amendment.[14]

This issue would seem equally arguable as to the terms of a public employer's drug testing policy negotiated with a union.

### 2. *Americans With Disabilities Act*

The tension between the law's *exclusion* of people currently engaged in illegal use of drugs from the scope of protection and its *inclusion* of people participating in a supervised rehabilitation program and no longer engaged in such use as within the Act's protection was addressed in *McDaniel v. Mississippi Baptist Medical Center.*[15] The plaintiff, a marketing representative for a hospital's chemical dependency center, reported

---

[13]*Id.* at 1570 (citing Bolden v. SEPTA, 953 F.2d 807, 7 IER Cases 92 (3d Cir. 1991), *cert. denied*, 504 U.S. 943 (1992)).

[14]Finkin, *The Limits of Majority Rule in Collective Bargaining*, 64 MINN. L. REV. 183, 253 (1980) (citing Lucas v. Colorado Gen. Assembly, 377 U.S. 713, 736–37 (1964)).

[15]877 F. Supp. 321 (S.D. Miss.), *aff'd*, 74 F.3d 1238 (5th Cir. 1995), after rulings on motion for summary judgment, 869 F. Supp. 445 (S.D. Miss. 1994).

his own drug abuse to his employer and, with his employer's encouragement, enrolled himself in a residential drug treatment program. Upon his return, he was given a "pink slip" that worked as either a termination or a reassignment.

Inasmuch as the plaintiff had been abusing lawful prescription drugs, a threshold question was whether he was engaged in "illegal use of drugs" within the exempting language. The court held he was, because the drugs were procured by fraud. Thus was the larger question presented and treated by the court:

> [T]he Act creates a "safe harbor" for chemically dependent persons who are participating in a supervised rehabilitation program and are no longer engaging in such use. As a practical matter, the question presents itself as to whether a chemically dependent person who is employed by a covered employer and who is currently engaging in illegal drug use, can escape termination by enrolling himself in a drug treatment program before he is caught by the employer.[16]

The court found, upon strongly conflicting facts, that the adverse employment action was conveyed to the employee before he entered treatment.

The court held in the alternative that even had the termination decision actually been made later, the employee was not covered by the exemption despite its literal application. The exemption requires not only admission to a rehabilitation program, but also successful completion and lack of further engagement in illegal drug use. Given the rate of relapse, especially in the first three months after treatment (and for as long as a year thereafter), the court read the Act to require recovery for a long enough period to indicate that the employee had "become stable."[17] Wherever that line is eventually to be drawn, it was not crossed here.

The court also held that the plaintiff was not a "qualified" individual under the Act (that is, for work that involved interviewing and interacting with young people with drug problems as a marketing representative for a rehabilitation program).[18] The employer argued that that function "at least from the standpoint of the public relations reputation of the facility" could not properly be performed by a relapsed representative.[19] The court agreed, despite the fact that the plaintiff secured employment in the drug treatment community and the court's observation that a substantial number of the defendant's employees were recovering chemically dependent people.[20]

---

[16] *Id.* at 326.
[17] *Id.* at 327–28.
[18] *Id.* at 328–29.
[19] *Id.* at 328.
[20] The court also held that the plaintiff had shown only minimal damages. *Id.* at 329.

## B. State Constitutional Constraints

The ordering of a drug test for an airline employee was challenged as an invasion of privacy under the California constitution.[21] The employee worked in equipment services, classified as a non-safety-sensitive position under a governing collective bargaining agreement. He had been ordered to take a drug test after his second accident in several weeks—an order he contested additionally as being racially motivated. The Eighth Circuit sustained the trial court's view that a drug test could be ordered out of safety concerns, the classification of the job by the collective bargaining agreement notwithstanding. Whether or not the actual order was justified by "reasonable suspicion" presented a fact question for the jury.[22]

## C. State Common Law Regulation: Employer Liability

### *1. Public Policy*

In *Gilmore v. Enogex, Inc.*,[23] the Supreme Court of Oklahoma confronted a challenge to a company's random drug testing policy based on public policy grounds including state and federal constitutional, statutory, and common law theories. The court rejected them all.

The plaintiff, an electrical engineer, had been employed by a company that had no drug testing policy but that was acquired by one that did. He refused to submit on grounds of privacy and was discharged. He then voluntarily secured a drug test that indicated the absence of drugs or alcohol, but to no avail. The court stressed the purpose of the company's policy:

> Employers have a legitimate interest in maintaining a work force free from the adverse effects of illegal drug and alcohol abuse. Safety issues and other concerns for efficiency prompted Enogex to take steps to ensure that its employees are neither intoxicated on the job nor performing under par because of off-duty drug and alcohol abuse. The means employed by Enogex' drug-testing policy, though perhaps intrusive, appear reasonably calculated to ensure this legitimate end. By announcing its Program several weeks before the actual testing, Enogex gave its employees an opportunity to cease current drug use so that they would not test positive when the Program was administered. The fact that the Program does not require dismissal of employees who tested positive, should they choose to undergo counseling, would indicate that Enogex intended not to replace its chemically dependent personnel, but rather to maintain a drug-free work environment.[24]

---

[21]Landon v. Northwest Airlines, 72 F.3d 620 (8th Cir. 1995).

[22]*Id.* at 625.

[23]878 P.2d 360, 9 IER Cases 1295 (Okla. 1994).

[24]*Id.* at 364 (footnote omitted).

On the privacy ground of the challenge, the court did hold the demand of a drug test to be so intrusive as to overcome any claim of consent, but it then held the intrusion not to be highly offensive to a reasonable person in view of the employer's legitimate interest in providing a drug-free workplace.

Inasmuch as the plaintiff was an electrical engineer, it remains to be seen how testing *him* was related to job safety (or efficiency). The Court does not suggest any such relationship. At that point the opinion becomes exceedingly fragile; that is, his refusal to consent to what the court concedes is an invasion of his privacy—on that very conscientiously held ground—was held to be justified by generalized concerns that do not implicate him either in view of his job or the actual state of his metabolites. What the policy requires, in other words, is obedience to an invasion of privacy for the sake of the policy.

The same approach was taken, if more perfunctorily, by the Ohio Court of Appeals in *Seta v. Reading Rock.*[25] The employee, an accountant, had been hired in 1986. In 1992, the company announced a drug testing policy. The employee, apparently a recreational marijuana user, failed a random drug test later that year and was discharged. The court held that neither the public policy of the state nor the employee's privacy had been violated. Citing prior authority, the court observed that a program designed to create a safe working environment does not violate a right to privacy.[26] It does not appear from the facts how an accountant posed such a threat to a safe working environment or whether she had so in fact threatened the safety of the working environment over the prior seven years of apparently satisfactory performance.

### *3. Defamation*

*d. Truth.* In *Washington v. Naylor Industrial Services,*[27] pursuant to a company's random drug testing policy no preliminary positive screen-

---

[25]654 N.E.2d 1061 (Ohio Ct. App. 1995).

[26]*Id,* at 1067, citing inter alia Groves v. Goodyear Tire & Rubber Co., 591 N.E.2d 875 (Ohio Ct. App. 1991).

[27]893 S.W.2d 309 (Tex. Ct. App. 1995). The policy provided in pertinent part:

> Once employed, all employees are subject to alcohol/drug screening at least annually on a random basis.
>
> All tests which are initially "negative" shall be deemed conclusive, and the employee shall not be subjected to further testing for the same incident, accident, suspicion, etc.
>
> All "positive" screens shall be confirmed by an independent and detailed chemical analysis. If such confirmation test results in a "negative" finding, the employee shall be conclusively deemed to have passed the screen. No positive screens are to be reported by any laboratory unless and until confirmed as above.

*Id.* at 310 n.1.

ing test (via an EMIT) was to be reported to the company; a confirming Gas Chromatography/Mass Spectrometry (GC/MS) test was required. However, after one employee failed an EMIT test, the laboratory informed the company's vice president, who ordered a confirming test and informed two of the employee's supervisors to reassign the employee to nonhazardous work pending the test result. The GC/MS was negative. The employee sued inter alia for defamation, but summary judgment for the company was affirmed on the ground of truth: "Regardless of how "failing" the drug test is defined, the objective truth is that [the employee] tested positive on the EMIT test. The laboratory's reporting of that fact may have breached [the employer's] policy of confidentiality, but its report was not false. . . ."[28] The defense of truth, being absolute, obviated the need to consider qualified privilege.

### *4. Infliction of Emotional Distress*

A mining foreman sought treatment for his drug and alcohol addiction and reported that fact to his employer (using his accumulated sick leave for the purpose of treatment).[29] Upon returning to work, he was required by the company to meet individually with each member of his work group to discuss their concerns about him. This requirement failed to establish a prima facie claim of emotional distress. A similar claim was not established when a company sent a report to an employee's supervisors that the employee had failed a screening test and issued an order to schedule him away from hazardous jobs.[30] In both cases, however, it should be noted that the employer's action was precautionary and related to legitimate safety concerns.

### *7. Individual Contract*

In *Robinson v. Utah Fuel Co.,*[31] the court read the employer's rules governing progressive discipline to be inapplicable to a demotion resulting from a supervisor's having sought drug rehabilitation. Neither the employer's drug policy—which assured only partial insurance coverage for such rehabilitative effort—nor informal and general assurances of management were held to constitute contractual commitments.

In *Washington v. Naylor Industrial Services,*[32] the court confronted the employer's breach of its own policy assuring confidentiality of drug test results. The court sustained the grant of summary judgment for the

[28] *Id.* at 311. *Accord,* Landon v. Northwest Airlines, 72 F.3d 620 (8th Cir. 1995).
[29] Robertson v. Utah Fuel Co., 889 P.2d 1382, 10 IER Cases 513 (Utah App. 1995).
[30] Washington v. Naylor Indus. Servs., 893 S.W.2d 309 (Tex. Ct. App. 1995).
[31] 889 P.2d 1382, 10 IER Cases 513 (Utah App. 1995).
[32] 893 S.W.2d 309 (Tex. Ct. App. 1995).

company on the ground that the company's "internal policies" do not constitute a contract:

> Naylor [the employer] was free to change its policy, abandon it, or make exceptions to it as it wished. For example, Naylor could have fired appellant, an employee at will, for the positive EMIT result, and he would have had no recourse, despite the policy. . . . If Naylor could have done that, it was certainly free to act as it did.[33]

The conclusion, however, rests on a non sequitur; that is, it does not follow that *because* the company could abandon the policy or discharge the employee without any cause it was free arbitrarily to make exceptions to the policy. The court supplied no reasoned ground as to why an express commitment to confidentiality would not have been binding on the employer, at least for as long as the policy remained in effect.

### *9. Physician and Laboratory Liability*

*a. Negligence.* In *Stinson v. Physicians Immediate Care, Ltd.,*[34] the appellate court of Illinois, following the weight of authority in other jurisdictions, held that a testing laboratory owed a duty of care to a tested employee such that negligence in the testing procedure would be actionable as a tort:

> The risk of harm in our society to an individual because of a false-positive drug test is so significant that failure to find protection under our law would be a step backwards for the protection of the individual. . . . [citing *Elliott v. Laboratory Specialists, Inc.,* 588 So. 2d 175 (La. App. 1991)]. "As information services become more prevalent in our economy and society, the information providers [, such as drug-testing laboratories,] should be held accountable for the information they provide. Such information should be complete and not misleading. Credit-reporting agencies have long been held to the exercise of due care in securing and distributing information concerning the financial standing of individuals, firms, and corporations." (*Doe v. SmithKline Beecham Corp.* (Tex. App. 1993), 855 S.W.2d 248, 255–56.) We agree with the *Elliott* and *Doe* courts that public policy requires the imposition of a duty here. The drug-testing laboratory is in the best position to guard against the injury, as it is solely responsible for the performance of the testing and the quality control procedures. In addition, the laboratory, which is paid to perform the tests, is better able to bear the burden financially than the individual wrongly maligned by a false positive report. We therefore hold that a drug-testing laboratory owes a duty of reasonable care to persons whose specimens it tests for employers or prospective employers.[35]

---

[33] *Id.* at 312.
[34] 646 N.E.2d 930, 10 IER Cases 756 (Ill. App. Ct. 1995).
[35] *Id.* at 934.

## E. Unemployment Compensation

Some states regulate employer drug testing policies indirectly, by use of workers' compensation and unemployment compensation laws. Both Alabama and Florida give workers' compensation premium discounts for employers who comply with drug-free workplace rules. (These recent statutes are set out in Part II of this supplement.) In addition, Florida establishes compliance with the testing requirements of the Act (laboratory certification, chain of custody rules, etc.), as creating a rebuttable presumption that an employee's positive test result is such misconduct as to deny unemployment compensation.[36] In the absence of evidence of such compliance, a positive drug test result would not alone be such misconduct as to deny benefits.[37]

# IV. NONWORK USE OF TOBACCO AND ALCOHOL[38]

## A. Constitutional Constraints

In *City of North Miami v. Kurtz*,[39] the Supreme Court of Florida sustained the city's prohibition on hiring employees who had used tobacco products for at least a year prior to applying for a job, against a challenge based on the Florida constitution's provision governing the right of privacy. The court acknowledged that the state's constitutional guaranty was broader than that recognized under the federal Constitution. Yet the Supreme Court of Florida approached the provision by a determination of the individual's "legitimate expectation of privacy" as has the U.S. Supreme Court in application of the Fourth Amendment:

> In today's society, smokers are constantly required to reveal whether they smoke. When individuals are seated in a restaurant, they are asked whether they want a table in a smoking or non-smoking section. When individuals rent hotel or motel rooms, they are asked if they smoke so that management may ensure that certain rooms remain free from the smell of smoke odors. Likewise, when individuals rent cars, they are asked if they smoke so that rental agencies can make proper accommodations to maintain vehicles for non-smokers. Further, employers generally provide smoke-free areas for non-smokers, and employees are often prohibited from smoking in certain areas. Given that individu-

---

[36]FLA. STAT. ANN. §443.101(11) (1996 Cum. Supp.).

[37]SKF Management v. Unemployment Appeal Comm'n, 664 So. 2d 345 (Fla. Dist. Ct. App. 1995).

[38]*See generally* Note, *Smoking Discrimination: Invading an Individual's Right to Privacy in the Home and Outside the Workplace?*, 21 OHIO N.U. L. REV. 1227 (1995); Ezra, *"Get Off Your Butts": The Employer's Right to Regulate Employee Smoking*, 60 TENN. L. REV. 905 (1993).

[39]653 So. 2d 1025, 10 IER Cases 865 (Fla. 1995).

> als must reveal whether they smoke in almost every aspect of life in today's society, we conclude that individuals have no reasonable expectation of privacy in the disclosure of that information when applying for a government job and, consequently, that Florida's right of privacy is not implicated under these unique circumstances.[40]

The analytical outset is curious in two regards: (1) all the actions listed are geared to the convenience of nonsmokers in the populace, not to the denial of employment, and (2) since private actions are not governed by the Florida constitution, as the court stressed, the court begs the question of why such private actions should drive the Florida constitution's public purpose.

The court then addressed the reasonableness of the job prohibition by pointing out that smoking tobacco is not considered a fundamental right under the federal Constitution. This reliance seems out of keeping with the court's observation at the outset that Florida's guaranty is broader than federal law. The court held the cost-driven reason for the prohibition to be reasonable, even to verge on the compelling: it found the record to reflect that "each smoking employee costs the City as much as $4,611 per year" over a nonsmoking employee—though no basis for this figure was given.[41] And the court noted, without seeing any inconsistency, that the means employed were the least intrusive inasmuch as the regulations did not prevent the retention of current smokers. Justice Kogen dissented, stating as follows:

> Health-based concerns like those expressed by the City also present a definite slippery slope to the courts. The time is fast approaching, for example, when human beings can be genetically tested so thoroughly that susceptibility to particular diseases can be identified years in advance. To my mind, any governmental effort to identify those who might eventually suffer from cancer or heart disease, for instance, itself is a violation of bodily integrity guaranteed by article I, section 23. Moreover, I cannot help but note that any such effort comes perilously close to the discredited practice of eugenics.[42]

## B. State Legislation Governing Nonwork Use of Tobacco and Alcohol

In *McEniry v. Landi,*[43] the New York Court of Appeals confronted the application of state law prohibiting discrimination on grounds of disability to an alcoholic employee who had been dismissed for alcoholism-related absences that occurred before he sought treatment. (He returned to work thereafter and performed satisfactorily.) The court held

---

[40]*Id.* at 1028.
[41]*Id.* at 1027.
[42]*Id.* at 1029 (Kogan, J., dissenting).
[43]644 N.E.2d 1019 (N.Y. 1994).

the determination of the employees' ability to perform must be made at the time of actual termination:

> Our holding is not intended to create a safe haven for individuals who resort to recovery programs as a pretext for avoiding otherwise legitimate disciplinary action, nor do we imply that in every case where an alcoholic is purportedly rehabilitated all disciplinary action is prohibited. The review is individualized. Thus, in the appropriate case, an alcoholic who is found not to be actually rehabilitated, or who is shown to have an established propensity to relapse may be found unable to perform the job in a reasonable manner. That was not the case here.[44]

[44] *Id.* at 1022 (citation omitted).

CHAPTER 3

# PSYCHOLOGICAL SCREENING AND TESTING

## I. POLYGRAPHY

### A. Constitutional Limits in Public Employment

In *Stehney v. Perry,*[1] an employee of a private, nonprofit think tank that performed sensitive research in cryptography for the federal National Security Agency was discharged by her employer because she had lost her security clearance. Her clearance had been terminated because she refused to submit to a polygraph examination authorized by the agency for the periodic reinvestigation of its contractors' personnel. She challenged the use of the polygraph on Fourth Amendment grounds.

The district court held that the use of a polygraph does not constitute a "search" within the meaning of the Fourth Amendment. After reviewing the cases dealing with voice and handwriting samples, fingerprints and dental examinations—criminal cases all—the court concluded:

> The incidental contact involved in attaching polygraph equipment and the rather innocuous readings of heart rate, respiration and perspiration changes are hardly more intrusive than a dental examination. *See United States v. Haynes*, 24 C.M.R. 881 (AFBR 1957) ("If there is anything hidden in the mind of the person subjected to such an examination, the machine does not produce it, though it appears to be evident that the examination and the results thereof are not infrequently cogent factors which lead the subject to reveal his secrets.").[2]

The court held in the alternative that the use of a polygraph was not unreasonable despite any psychological stress its use produced, and however annoying, frightening, and perhaps humiliating it may be, especially in light of the national security interests at stake.

The latter reasoning may be more supportable than the former, for the court's treatment of the issue in terms of physical intrusion alone rather assumes the real issue. What is "produced" by the use of the machine are not secrets hidden in the mind (if the proponents of polygraphy are to be credited), but one's state of mind, and so the real question in Fourth Amendment terms is whether a probing of one's mind in that

[1]907 F. Supp. 806 (D.N.J. 1995).
[2]*Id.* at 823.

regard by technical means works a "search" even if no mechanical (or chemical) intrusion is involved.

## B. The Federal Employee Polygraph Protection Act

### *1. Employer Liability Under the EPPA*

The employer's motion for summary judgment in *Lyle v. Mercy Hospital Anderson*[3] raised two separate statutory questions. The first issue concerned whether the hospital had requested that an employee submit to a polygraph. The hospital had commenced an investigation after several surgery personnel had reported thefts from their lockers. The plaintiff, a surgical assistant, had had access to the surgical locker room at the time in question and could not clarify his precise whereabouts at the time of the theft. The hospital's vice president for human resources, who was conducting the investigation, mentioned the possibility of a lie detector in a meeting with the staff and allegedly asked the plaintiff how he felt about a lie detector. A written comment entered after a search of the employee's locker noted "objected to polygraph," and the vice president's report stated that the plaintiff had not expressed interest in taking a lie detector test, whereas the others had. The hospital argued that the plaintiff had failed to make out a prima facie case that the hospital had required, requested, or caused the plaintiff to take a lie detector test within the meaning of the Act. All he was asked was whether he would be willing to take a test if offered. The court disagreed:

> A reasonable juror viewing plaintiff's version of the events and the record as a whole could reasonably conclude that Finley [the vice president] directly or indirectly suggested to plaintiff that he needed to take a lie detector test or that Finley based his decision to discharge plaintiff on his unwillingness to submit to a lie detector test.[4]

The second issue concerned the exemption that allows the use of a polygraph "administered in connection with an ongoing investigation involving economic loss or injury to the employer's business, such as theft, embezzlement, misappropriation. . . ."[5] The hospital argued to regulations of the Department of Labor dealing with "indirect loss" including theft of property for which the employee exercises fiduciary, managerial, or security responsibility, such as a building manager's theft of property from rental apartments.[6] The court disagreed:

> Arguably, the theft from the doctor was unrelated to the hospital's main business of patient care, and therefore Mercy Hospital suffered no indirect

---

[3]876 F. Supp. 157, 10 IER Cases 401 (S.D. Ohio 1995).

[4]*Id.* at 160.

[5]29 C.F.R. §801.12(a)(1).

[6]*Id.* §801(c)(1)(iv) (*see* main volume at p. 185).

> loss to its business of providing patient care. The apartment manager's business is essentially accepting money (lease payments) in exchange for providing tenants with a safe and secure place to live. This business suffers a loss when a maintenance employee steals from a tenant. Mercy Hospital, in contrast, has not demonstrated under the rules applied on summary judgment how its main business of patient care suffered a loss because of the theft . . . .[7]

Moreover, inasmuch as the hospital had claimed the exemption, it was bound by the procedural safeguards attendant to a permitted use, which it did not observe.

The EPPA regulates only employers, defined to include those who act directly or indirectly in their interest with regard to an employee. Where a union officer suggested to an employee discharged for theft that the employer might be willing to reinstate him if the employee was willing to take (and pass) a polygraph examination, and the union officer negotiated with the employer to secure that agreement, the officer was not covered by the EPPA as one acting in the employer's interest.[8]

### *2. Polygrapher Liability Under the EPPA*

The court in *Rubin v. Tourneau, Inc.*,[9] judged polygrapher liability according to whether or not the polygrapher was acting directly or indirectly in the interest of the employer (i.e., the polygrapher was not liable if subject to the employer's direction and control, but was liable if acting on independent judgment in selecting the employees to be examined or the like). This analysis has been followed—in one case to grant summary judgment for the polygrapher,[10] and in another to hold that the issue was one of fact.[11]

## II. PERSONALITY TESTING

Additional literature is noted below.[12]

## III. HONESTY AND INTEGRITY TESTING

Additional literature is noted below.[13]

---

[7]876 F. Supp. at 161.

[8]del Canto v. ITT Sheraton Corp., 865 F. Supp. 927, 9 IER Cases 1809 (D.D.C. 1994), *aff'd*, 70 F.3d 637 (D.C. Cir. 1995).

[9]797 F. Supp. 247, 7 IER Cases 993 (S.D.N.Y. 1992).

[10]Fallin v. Mindis Metals, Inc., 865 F. Supp. 834 (N.D. Ga. 1994).

[11]James v. Professionals' Detective Agency, 876 F. Supp. 1013, 10 IER Cases 590 (N.D. Ill. 1995).

[12]Black, *Personality Screening in Employment*, 32 AM. BUS. L.J. 69 (1994).

[13]Yamada, *The Regulation of Pre-Employment Honesty Testing: Striking a Temporary (?) Balance Between Self-Regulation and Prohibition*, 39 WAYNE L. REV. 1549 (1993); Metzger & Dalton, *"Just Say No" to Integrity Testing*, 4 U. FLA. J.L. & PUB. POL'Y 9 (1991).

## V. REQUIRED EMPLOYEE SUBMISSION TO PSYCHOLOGICAL EVALUATION

The privilege of an employer to request an employee to submit to a psychological examination upon an adequate showing of a reasonable reason for the request, and to discharge the employee for refusal to comply, was discussed in *Marquart v. McDonnell Douglas Corp.,*[14] a Title VII case:

> Time and again, plaintiff displayed abnormal behavior at work. Prior psychiatric examination in 1990 had resulted in evaluations that she needed treatment. Defendant's company physician directed that plaintiff make herself available for further diagnosis. Plaintiff refused to cooperate in this regard and was told that she must submit to examination by a psychiatrist or be terminated from her employment. Plaintiff was unwilling to keep appointments with physicians which had been made for her. Ultimately, she did appear with a friend at the office of Dr. David Goldmeier but was totally uncooperative and refused to sign a release for records to be sent to defendant's physician or allow an examination. Although plaintiff contends that Dr. Goldmeier was abusive, plaintiff's friend, Bernice Fair, who at plaintiff's insistence had accompanied her into the doctor's office and was with her when the doctor tried to examine her, related that he had been "very nice."
>
> . . . .
>
> The Court finds that plaintiff did indeed exhibit irrational and bizarre behavior at work and that defendant's request that she submit herself for evaluation and treatment was reasonable.[15]

Likewise, in *Flynn v. Sandahl,*[16] the U.S. Court of Appeals for the Seventh Circuit held that a public employer may demand that an employee submit to a psychiatric examination upon a "demonstrated . . . justifiable basis"—in that case, reports by coworkers that the employee had threatened them with physical harm.[17] Analogously, it has been held that a workers' compensation insurance carrier can withhold payments if an employee refuses a reasonable request to be examined by a rehabilitation counselor.[18]

---

[14]859 F. Supp. 366 (E.D. Mo. 1994), *aff'd,* 56 F.3d 69 (8th Cir. 1995).

[15]*Id.* at 369. On the reasonableness of state law allowing a medical licensing board to require a physician to submit to a psychiatric evaluation as a condition of retention of the medical license, see Humenansky v. Minnesota Bd. of Medical Examiners, 525 N.W.2d 559 (Minn. Ct. App. 1994).

[16]58 F.3d 283, 10 IER Cases 1187 (7th Cir. 1995).

[17]*Id.* at 290.

[18]Steward v. Matthews Indus., 644 So. 2d 915 (Ala. 1994).

CHAPTER 4

# INTERVIEW QUESTIONS, QUESTIONNAIRES, CREDIT CHECKS, AND REFERENCES

## I. APPLICATIONS AND INTERVIEWS

### B. Questions and Questionnaires: Private Sector

Although no case has yet held a right of privacy to apply to a question asked of an applicant in a job interview, the individual's right of informational self-determination has been partially protected—but only indirectly—when the nature of an inquiry is thought to implicate some other societal end, most often nondiscrimination in employment.

A different theory was pursued in *Tomsic v. State Farm Mutual Automobile Insurance Co.*[1] A job trainee sued for sex discrimination and infliction of emotional distress when her supervisor/trainer asked her how her husband would feel in several years when she would be making more money than he. (The husband had previously applied for the job and been denied.) The trainer testified that he had had a problem with another female trainee for that very reason and was concerned that the same might happen here—especially because the wife had gotten the job the husband wanted. The court held that asking the question did not give rise to a cause of action: it did not constitute outrageous conduct of the kind covered by that tort.

#### *1. Truthfulness*

As the main volume pointed out, the common assumption is that an applicant (or employee) owes a duty of candor to the employer such that an untruthful answer would be good reason for discharge. In the absence of a statutory prohibition on the question being asked, little or no attention has been devoted to whether a specific question is one to which a reply was due. The issue has cropped up in employment discrimination law where an employer's investigation of a complaining employee has unearthed an apparent misrepresentation upon which, it was alleged, the employee could independently have been discharged.

[1]870 F. Supp. 318 (D. Utah 1994).

In *McKennon v. Nashville Banner Publishing Co.*,[2] the U.S. Supreme Court confronted this issue in a case arising under the Age Discrimination in Employment Act in which the employer learned of arguable misconduct during the complainant's employment. The Court concluded that "after-acquired evidence of wrongdoing which would have resulted in discharge" does not bar the employee from all statutory relief.[3] The case is relevant here insofar as it would require inquiry into the materiality of a misrepresentation made during the hiring process, but only as to statutory discriminatees. The pertinent inquiry would be whether the misrepresentation would have resulted in discharge upon discovery,[4] which the Fourth Circuit has characterized as actually a case of "after-acquired motive" rather than of after-acquired evidence:

> In such cases, the employer does not assert that it had in its mind a legitimate nondiscriminatory reason that explains its challenged action and that would insulate it, to whatever extent, as in the mixed-motive case; instead, the employer argues that it has acquired evidence since the time of that action that, had it known it at the time, would have led it to do exactly what it did, except for a legitimate reason rather than an illegal one.[5]

Consequently, whether or not there was a misrepresentation and the materiality of the alleged misrepresentation are subjects of litigation. In the *Microdyne* case, the employee had been working part-time for another company at the time of her application for full-time employment, and she had annualized her part-time rate upon the employer's inquiry as to her current salary.[6] Whether or not this constituted a misrepresentation, and if so, whether it would have caused the company not to hire her had it known at the time, were held to be fact issues that precluded summary judgment.[7]

Where an employee is under a contract of a stated term, or an employer is governed by a contractually binding commitment not to discharge except for good or just cause, a discharge on grounds of misrepresentation in the hiring process would also have to meet a test of materiality. But absent a plaintiff with a contract or a prima facie claim of employment discrimination, the employment is at will and the employee may be dismissed on a ground of untruthfulness without any need to demonstrate the fact or its materiality.[8]

---

[2]115 S. Ct. 879 (1995).

[3]*Id.* at 883.

[4]Wallace v. Dunn Constr. Co., 62 F.3d 374 (11th Cir. 1995) (reviewing authority).

[5]Russell v. Microdyne Corp., 65 F.3d 1229, 1237 (4th Cir. 1995).

[6]*Id.*

[7]*Id.* In Camp v. Jeffer, Mangels, Butler & Marmaro, 41 Cal. Rptr. 2d 329 (Cal. Ct. App. 1995), the failure of the plaintiff-employees to have truthfully informed their prospective employer of their felony convictions was held to be material—and disqualifying of any relief—given the nature of the job.

[8]DePluzer v. Village of Winnetka, 638 N.E.2d 1157, 9 IER Cases 1310 (Ill. App. Ct. 1994).

However, the question of the materiality of the misrepresentation is not quite the same as the question of whether the inquiry is one that ought to be allowed. In the Federal Republic of Germany, for example, the individual's right of informational self-determination has been held to apply to questions concerning an applicant's previous remuneration unless the applicant claims it as a floor for future pay or it is of importance to the position sought.[9] And if a question is impermissible, it would not be grounds for termination if the individual lied in response to it.[10]

*Georgia Electric Co. v. Rycroft*[11] concerned the law of workers' compensation, where it has been held that a misrepresentation will cause a denial of benefits only if the misrepresentation concerns the employee's physical condition at the time of hire *and* was causally related to the inquiry that was the subject of the dispute.[12]

## II. CREDIT CHECKS

### E. Statutory Liability

In *Weir v. Equifax Services, Inc.*,[13] a disappointed applicant sued his former employer and a credit rating service for defamation. The court did not mention federal law, inquiring only as to any evidence of actual ill will or reckless disregard for the truth that would defeat the qualified privilege that attaches to such communications. The credit rating service's "confidential report" indicated that the applicant, an insurance sales representative, had left his prior employer "owing it about $6,000; that there had been numerous charge backs against his accounts because policies were canceled shortly after commissions had been paid; that plaintiff had falsified records on applications for insurance policies on his own family and himself; and that there [was] litigation pending between plaintiff and" the prior employer.[14] The court found no triable facts in issue to sustain the plaintiff's claim of abuse of the privilege.

## III. BACKGROUND CHECKS

In one case a disappointed applicant sued his would-be employer on the ground that its having contacted his prior employer for a reference

[9]G. HALLBACH et al., LABOUR LAW IN GERMANY: AN OVERVIEW 49 (A. Haarkamp et al. trans., 4th rev'd ed. 1991).

[10]*Id.*

[11]378 S.E.2d 111 (Ga. 1989).

[12]*Id.*

[13]620 N.Y.S.2d 675 (App. Div. 1994).

[14]*Id.* at 676.

constituted an impermissible conflict of interest.[15] The court rejected the assertion.[16]

## A. Actionable Defamation and Inactionable Opinion

Some jurisdictions, such as Illinois, adhere to the "innocent construction" rule whereby an allegedly defamatory statement will not be regarded as defamatory if it can reasonably be interpreted as lacking in defamatory content. In *Anderson v. Vanden Dorpel,*[17] for example, a prospective employer inquired regarding the applicant's performance with her current employer. The applicant's supervisor told the inquirer that the applicant "could not get along with her co-workers" and "did not follow-up on assignments."[18] The court held, reviewing authority, that the former statement was capable of being given an innocent construction, but that the latter went to the core of her job as a corporate fundraiser for a private university and was defamatory.

In *Marcoux-Norton v. Kmart Corp.,*[19] an employee had applied for a loan from a bank which in turn contacted the current employer. Upon consulting with the employee's supervisor (with whom the employee was having serious difficulties), the responsible officer replied on the bank's form, under "probability of continued employment," "50-50 at this time."[20] In response to the employer's motion for summary judgment, the court opined:

> It is for the trier of fact to determine whether Kmart's answer of "50-50" in response to an inquiry regarding Plaintiff's likelihood of continued employment would indicate to a respectable community that everyone's chances of continued employment are 50-50, or whether such a statement would instead indicate to this respectable community that Plaintiff performed his job poorly and therefore had as much likelihood of continuing his employment as he had of being terminated.[21]

Likewise, in *Free v. American Home Assurance Co.,*[22] a former supervisor's statements to a corporate headhunter, indicating that a former employee was a "lightweight" who "lacked a comprehensive grasp of what was necessary to handle large accounts," failed to follow through,

---

[15]Booth v. Total Health Care, Inc., 880 F. Supp. 414 (D. Md. 1994), *aff'd*, 48 F.3d 1215 (4th Cir. 1995).

[16]*See generally* Note, *Contracting Around the Law of Defamation and Employment References*, 79 VA. L. REV. 517 (1993).

[17]645 N.E.2d 250 (Ill. App. Ct. 1994).

[18]*Id.* at 253.

[19]907 F. Supp. 766, 10 IER Cases 1768 (D. Vt. 1993).

[20]*Id.* at 770.

[21]*Id.* at 779 (footnote omitted).

[22]902 S.W.2d 51 (Tex. Ct. App. 1995).

and would procrastinate, were held to charge the former employee with professional incompetence and so stated a claim in defamation.[23]

## B. Abuse of Privilege in Defamation, Privacy, or Interference in Prospective Economic Relationships

*Anderson v. Vanden Dorpel*[24] recognized that a conditional privilege attaches to references supplied by a prior or current employer to a prospective one, and so the question presented was of abuse of the privilege by either an intention to injure or reckless disregard of the truth. In that case, the employer's Staff Handbook provided that the employer would only verify an employee's dates of employment, job title, and salary, and that this information would be provided only with the employee's written authorization (which was not given). The trial court's grant of the employer's motion to dismiss was reversed:

> The complaint alleges that plaintiff had received exemplary job performance reviews during her nine years of employment, that Vanden Dorpel knew that the university's handbook did not allow him to give employment information about plaintiff without her permission, and that Vanden Dorpel made false statements about plaintiff's work performance to Crown.
>
> Vanden Dorpel's statements can be considered as a disregard for plaintiff's rights. Further proceedings may prove that Vanden Dorpel knew or should have known that it was improper under the university's policies to disclose any information about an employee over the telephone. Furthermore, plaintiff may be able to prove that Vanden Dorpel should not have given information about her without first ascertaining whether she gave prior written authorization to do so. Thus, defendants may have abused any conditional privilege they had.[25]

Likewise, a federal district court applying Vermont law held that a conditional privilege applies to a credit reference given by a current employer, but that it was a fact question for the jury whether the statement was made with knowledge of or in disregard of its falsity, or was made with an intent to injure.[26]

## C. Authorization or Consent

In *Cox v. Nasche,*[27] the Ninth Circuit was called upon to decide whether Alaska law would accord an absolute or a conditional privilege to information given by a prior employer to the Federal Aviation Adminis-

---

[23] *Id.* at 53, 54.
[24] 645 N.E.2d 250 (Ill. App. Ct. 1994).
[25] *Id.* at 259.
[26] Marcoux-Norton v. Kmart Corp., 907 F. Supp. 766, 10 IER Cases 1768 (D. Vt. 1993).
[27] 70 F.3d 1030, 11 IER Cases 281 (9th Cir. 1995).

tration concerning the applicant's prior employment. The applicant signed a release providing in pertinent part:

> *AUTHORITY FOR RELEASE OF INFORMATION*
>
> I Authorize any duly accredited representative of the Federal Government . . . to obtain any information relating to my activities from . . . employers. . . . This information may include, but is not limited to, . . . achievement, performance, attendance, personal history, disciplinary . . . information.
>
> I Direct You to Release such information upon request of the duly accredited representative of any authorized agency regardless of any agreement I may have made with you previously to the contrary.
>
> I Release any individual, including records custodians, from all liability for damages that may result to me on account of compliance or any attempts to comply with this authorization.[28]

After reviewing the law from several jurisdictions (which included some conflicts), and in view of the sensitive nature of the job applied for (Aviation Safety Inspector), the court concluded that an absolute privilege would apply to statements made so long as they were within the scope of the release.[29]

The question of consent was raised when an employee's loan application included a waiver for information provided by his current employer.[30] The trial court held that it was a fact question whether or not the employee reasonably should have anticipated a defamatory response and, if he had, whether he would have consented to it.

The same approach was taken to the defense of "invitation."[31] Where a former employee retained a corporate headhunter who, in turn, contacted the client's former supervisor for a reference, the employer argued that the former employee should be taken to have invited the allegedly defamatory reference. The employee had submitted a letter of resignation recounting his difficulties with his supervisor, Mr. Boyd.[32] The court held that though

---

[28] *Id.* at 1030–31.

[29] *Per contra* Kellums v. Freight Sales Ctrs., Inc., 467 So. 2d 816 (Fla. App. 1985).

[30] Marcoux-Norton v. Kmart Corp., 907 F. Supp. 766, 10 IER Cases 1768 (D. Vt. 1995), *following* McDermott v. Hughley, 561 A.2d 1038 (Md. 1989).

[31] Free v. American Home Assurance Co., 902 S.W.2d 51 (Tex. Ct. App. 1995).

[32] It provided in pertinent part:

> Mr. Boyd started asking me about the status of the various audits I was working on. These files were not in one central location so I began to move about my office to retrieve these files while attempting to continue my conversation with Mr. Boyd. When he came to an audit file by the name of Ivex Packaging, Mr. Boyd claims that instead of requesting the status of the file he asked if I had been out to the insureds the morning of the 18th. I understood him to be asking the same as he had been on all the other files and proceeded to give him the status of the audit to date. When Mr. Boyd got what he thought was an affirmative answer to his question concerning my location the morning of the 18th he called Mr. Denis Sucec at Ivex to confirm. Mr. Sucec told him I had not been there the morning of the 18th.

*Id.* at 55.

the letter gave reason to believe that Boyd, if contacted, would not speak favorably of the employee, it did not establish that the employee knew in advance that his former supervisor would say what he did.

## D. Employee Republication

The question of whether a foreseeable reiteration by an applicant of the reasons given by his or her employer for the employee's termination works a "publication" of the statement, and so gives rise to potential liability if the statement was defamatory, continues to vex the courts. The Tenth Circuit, predicting Oklahoma law (and reviewing authority), concluded that a "small number of other jurisdictions" have adopted the self-publication doctrine, and then itself rejected it.[33] It also opined, however, that the theory could not have availed the plaintiff in any event: there was no evidence that she was forced to repeat the employer's allegation of the basis for the discharge, and the allegation, of a failure to cooperate in the employer's investigation of a theft, was true. However, a federal district court in Arkansas, predicting that state's law, held the allegation of self-publication to survive a motion to dismiss.[34]

An intermediate appellate court in Illinois declined to allow the theory in part on the ground that new causes of action should be created by the legislature or the state supreme court.[35] A federal district court in New York noted that the theory had been accepted in two federal districts in the state and rejected in one,[36] but the court obviated the need to decide the question. It held the theory inapplicable to an allegation of employee misconduct that the former employer had made in an unemployment compensation hearing. The statement had not been made in the context of the employee's termination, but only months later as a reason to deny unemployment compensation; thus the former employee could not labor under any foreseeable compulsion to repeat that statement to a prospective employer.

The District of Columbia Court of Appeals predicted that Virginia would not accept the self-publication theory.[37] The court noted that only a minority of jurisdictions had accepted the theory, and that those that had

---

[33]Starr v. Pearle Vision, Inc., 54 F.3d 1548 (10th Cir. 1995). Inasmuch as Wisconsin has held that actions against employers in defamation are precluded by the state's workers' compensation act, the Wisconsin Court of Appeals held that that preclusion would apply as well to any theory of self-publication. Wolf v. F & M Banks, 534 N.W.2d 877, 10 IER Cases 827 (Wis. Ct. App. 1995).

[34]Coatney v. Enterprise Rent-A-Car Co., 897 F. Supp. 1205, 11 IER Cases 628 (W.D. Ark. 1995).

[35]Harrel v. Dillards Dep't Stores, 644 N.E.2D 448 (Ill. App. Ct. 1994).

[36]Chrzanowski v. Lichtman, 884 F. Supp. 751 (W.D.N.Y. 1995).

[37]Atkins v. Industrial Telecommunications Ass'n, 660 A.2d 885 (D.C. 1995).

rejected it did so because either (1) there was no element of compulsion (presumably in contradistinction to foreseeability) present in the particular case, or (2) "a causal link between the action of the originator and the damage caused by the publication" was absent.[38]

The latter factor was dwelt on in an opinion of Judge Posner observing, in dictum, that *had* the issue been presented, the court *would have* predicted that Illinois would reject what he characterized as an "absurdity," the doctrine of "self-defamation."[39] The doctrine, he opined, gives an employee a "surrogate" for a contract of employment that the employee has not in fact secured.[40] As he explained, "it makes it impossible for an employer to communicate his grounds for discharging an employee to the employee even confidentially without incurring a grave risk of being sued for defamation."[41]

As the universal recognition of a qualified privilege extending to background checks evidences—and as the recent statutory development outlined in the next subsection emphasizes—the policy of the law is to encourage the sharing of information concerning an applicant or prospective employee's performance, but subject to a duty of care that the information has not been gathered or stated in reckless disregard for the truth. It remains to be seen why an employer should be able to avoid that standard of care by informing only the employee of a wrongful ground of discharge determined in reckless disregard for the truth. It is difficult to see how that action, predicated on the foreseeability of being required to state the reason given by the prior employer for discharge, is a surrogate for a contract of employment. In a contract case, the burden of proof rests on the employer to prove not a reasonable belief founded on an adequate investigation of the facts, but that the facts demonstrate cause to discharge to a jury's satisfaction. In *Rice v. Nova Biomedical Corp.*,[42] the fact that the plaintiff was able to secure a better paying job almost immediately, though not doctrinally inconsistent with damages for reputational harm, could have been taken to evidence that that harm was no more than nominal.

A federal district court in Maine,[43] upon a thorough review of the case law elsewhere, concluded that Maine would recognize the theory as applicable in cases where the former employee would be required to restate the reason given by the employer for the employee's leaving employment. In the employment context, the court opined, "job applicants

[38] *Id.* at 894.
[39] Rice v. Nova Biomedical Corp., 38 F.3d 909, 911 (7th Cir. 1994).
[40] *Id.* at 912.
[41] *Id.*
[42] 38 F.3d 909 (7th Cir. 1994).
[43] Carey v. Mt. Desert Island Hosp., 910 F. Supp. 7 (D. Me. 1995).

often wield little power in the interviewing process, and in certain situations they must republish defamatory statements in order to satisfy prospective employers."[44] And, it noted, unlike in a situation involving repetition to a family member or friend, "[i]n the context of employment the plaintiff-employee is under economic pressure to find another job, and as such can be said to be strongly compelled to publish the defamatory statement. Lying is not an acceptable alternative to republication."[45]

So, too, has the Oregon Court of Appeals in *Downs v. Waremart.*[46] Contrary to some of the authority just reviewed, the court comprehensively surveyed the law and concluded that of the 20 courts to have considered the question a slight majority had recognized the doctrine. It chose to join them:

> We do so for two reasons. First, an employer who knowingly or recklessly makes false statements about a former employee to that person's prospective employer can be liable for defamation. . . . We see no reason why an employer who knowingly or recklessly gives an employee a defamatory reason for his or her discharge, when it is reasonably foreseeable that the employee will be under a strong compulsion to disclose that reason to putative employers, should be treated any differently. Causation and harm in both instances are the same. To impose liability in the first, but not the second, would elevate form over substance; it would permit employers to achieve indirectly that which they cannot do directly.
>
> Second, . . . a defendant who makes defamatory statements to a third party is liable not only for that publication, but also for the third party's reasonably foreseeable republication of those statements to others. Again, . . . we see no reason why the same principle should not apply equally "where the foreseeable republication is made by the person defamed operating under a strong compulsion to republish the defamatory statement and the circumstances that create the strong compulsion are known to the originator of the defamatory statement at the time he communicates it to the person defamed."[47]

It stressed, as have other courts,[48] that the qualified privilege that attaches to a former employer's statements to a prospective one attaches as well to an applicant's republication.

## E. Statutory Regulation of References

Eleven states have legislated to confer a statutory privilege to communications made by current or past employers to prospective employers concerning employees, most enacted in the past two or three years.[49]

---

[44]*Id.* at 12.

[45]*Id.* at 12 n.3.

[46]903 P.2d 888 (Or. Ct. App. 1995), *review allowed,* 909 P.2d 161 (Or. 1996).

[47]*Id.* at 895–96.

[48]*See* Bickling v. Kent Gen. Hosp., 872 F. Supp. 1299 (D. Del. 1994).

[49]A complete text of these statutes is set out in Part II of this Supplement.

These laws are intended to encourage such references to be given, largely by codifying that a qualified privilege attaches to them. There is, however, a significant distinction in the way some of these statutes are drafted. Alaska, Arizona, and Tennessee grant a presumption that such communications are made in good faith, but allow the presumption to be defeated by proof that the utterance was made recklessly, was knowingly false, or was made with a malicious purpose. But Florida, Indiana, Louisiana, New Mexico, and Utah omit recklessness as a ground to rebut the privilege, thus narrowing the scope of potential liability. Maine follows the latter approach, but states that the provision is "supplemental to and not in derogation of any claims available to the former employee" under state law.[50] The most sharply focused of these laws is Iowa's. It extends a qualified immunity to such communications generally; but it extends absolute immunity for the disclosure of (1) date of employment, (2) pay level, (3) job description and duties, and (4) wage history. It also extends absolute immunity to the following information to which the employee has or had access (presumable under Iowa's employee access to records law):

> (1) Written employee evaluations which were conducted prior to the employee's separation from the employer and to which an employee shall be given a copy upon request; and
> (2) whether the employee was voluntarily or involuntarily released from service and the reasons for the separation.[51]

Illinois took the second of the approaches outlined above—according a rebuttable presumption for "good faith" statements about a prior employee's job performance but allowing that presumption to be rebutted by proof that the statement was made with knowledge of falsity "or in violation of a civil right."[52] [The action occurred as this book went to press. The full text will be added to the 1997 supplement to *Privacy in Employment Law.*]

---

[50] ME. REV. STAT. ANN. tit. 26, §598 (West 1995).
[51] IOWA CODE §1(c)(1)–(2) (1995).
[52] P.L. 89-470, Ill. Laws of 1996.

CHAPTER 5

# MONITORING EMPLOYEE PERFORMANCE AND CONDUCT

## II. INVESTIGATION

### A. Interrogation

As in the law of applicant interviews discussed in the preceding chapter, the common assumption is that an incumbent employee owes a duty to cooperate in any investigation, which includes a duty of truthfulness in replying to questions. Again, there is scant attention to the issue of whether a question is one that the employer is permitted to ask and, if not, whether the duty of candor extends to such a question.

The issue was presented to the National Labor Relations Board in *Earle Industries.*[1] The complaining employee had participated in an in-plant protest that the employer had on videotape from a local television station. The employer interrogated the employee about the incident. At first she refused to answer, but on being informed that failure to cooperate was a violation of the company's rules, she lied about her activities and was discharged. The two-member Board majority held the discharge violative of the Labor Act, stating that her activity in the protest was statutorily protected. According to the Board, although the "interrogation was not alleged to have independently violated the Act," the employee was under "no obligation to 'cooperate' " with it. Consequently, her lies in answer to the questions could not supply an independent ground of termination. The dissenting Board member opined to the contrary: If the company had a right to inquire of the employee's activities in the incident, as it did, the employee had a duty to answer truthfully. The Eighth Circuit agreed with the dissenting member, but even here Judge Wollman dissented on the ground that the Board could find protected false statements uttered during the course of statutorily protected activity.[2]

---

[1]315 NLRB No. 45 (1994), *enforcement denied*, 75 F.3d 400 (8th Cir. 1996).
[2]75 F.3d at 408.

### *1. Representation During Interrogation*

In *TRW, Inc. v. Superior Court (MA),*[3] a physicist employed by a defense contractor was summoned to an investigative interview concerning the possibility of a breach in security. He refused to attend unless accompanied by his lawyer and was subsequently terminated for insubordination. The court held that no public policy was breached by the discharge and that the contractor's relationship to the government was not such as to cause the Fifth or Fourth Amendment to apply.

A more complex situation was presented in *White v. Health Midwest Development Group.*[4] There a secretary had been reinstated in settlement of an employment discrimination claim negotiated with her lawyer, the terms of which included provision for her precise job responsibilities. When the employer insisted that she agree to perform certain duties, she refused to accept, pending consultation with her lawyer over whether or not those duties were covered by the settlement agreement, and she was discharged. The court held she had no right to counsel prior to performing the assigned task:

> The creation of such a right would produce impractical results, particularly in a situation where the requested task is neither dangerous nor illegal. Allowing employees the right to consult with an attorney every time they had a doubt about the propriety of an assigned task would substantially hinder an employer's operation. As suggested by the defendant, it would "in effect transfer decision-making power from the [employer] to their employees' attorneys." This is a proposition which this court cannot approve. Plaintiff's remedy in this case, if she believed that the assigned tasks violated the parties' agreement, would have been to perform the tasks and then bring an action against the defendant for declaratory relief.[5]

### *2. Abusive Interrogation*

An employee of a drug treatment and rehabilitation center had been reported by patients as using cocaine; their allegation was investigated by the center's management.[6] Management representatives then met with the employee and, in light of his prior drug addiction, requested that he submit to a drug test, which he agreed to do. They then canceled the test, over his objection. He complained of the denial of his right to clear himself and attempted, unsuccessfully, to arrange for a urinalysis. It was later suggested to him that he ought to transfer to another position. None of this amounted to the tort of emotional distress: the court held that the

---

[3] 31 Cal. Rptr. 2d 460 (Cal. Ct. App. 1994).

[4] 889 F. Supp. 1439 (D. Kan. 1995).

[5] *Id.* at 1445.

[6] Thomas v. St. Luke's Health Sys., Inc., 869 F. Supp. 1413 (N.D. Iowa, 1994), *aff'd*, 61 F.3d 908 (8th Cir. 1995).

employer had taken "reasonable steps to investigate" the allegation of drug use.[7]

In another case, an interview, conducted in the presence of a security guard, in which an employee was asked to explain discrepancies between her timesheets and the company's security entries for her times of arrival was held not to have inflicted emotional distress.[8] Other courts have failed to find emotional distress in situations involving a 45-minute interview conducted off the company's premises by three executives;[9] a day-long investigation of an employee (for operating a business on company time) during which several hours were spent in an interrogation (in the presence of a union representative) in which the interrogator engaged in a certain amount of sarcasm, ridicule, teasing, and taunting;[10] an interrogation of a manager to explain a report of wrongdoing;[11] and an investigation of allegedly sexually harassing behavior by a supervisor in the course of which the company's investigating official said to the employee (1) that the employee "might as well have been a murderer, rapist, or child molester," (2) as to provocative and sexual remarks by the female employee, that "if [she] pulled her pants down and you would have looked, you were just as guilty," and (3) as to the employee's profession of innocence, that "you don't have to get your hand wet to be guilty."[12]

A more vexing set of facts was presented in *Downs v. Waremart,*[13] where an employee, suspected of attempted theft, was interrogated by a police detective in the workplace and in the presence of a company manager. The suspect/employee had been read her *Miranda* rights but continued the interrogation nevertheless at the manager's instruction. When she asked to have an attorney present, the police ceased the interrogation and she called her lawyer. She was terminated later that morning, as her manager put it, in light of her having called her lawyer. Her discharge on that account was held not to violate the public policy of the state.

### *3. False Imprisonment*

The conduct of an interview, even for a prolonged period of time, in which the employee's presence is assured not by force or the threat

---

[7] *Id.* at 1441.

[8] Olmstead v. Federated Dep't Stores, 617 N.Y.S.2d 225 (App. Div. 1994). *See also* Downs v. Waremart, 903 P.2d 888 (Or. App. 1995), *review allowed,* 909 P.2d 161 (Or. 1996).

[9] State Farm Mut. Auto. Ins. Co. v. Novotny, 657 So. 2d 1210 (Fla. Dist. Ct. App. 1995).

[10] Trahan v. Bellsouth Telecommunications, Inc., 881 F. Supp. 1080 (W.D. La.), *aff'd,* 71 F.3d 876 (5th Cir. 1995).

[11] Randall's Food Mkts., Inc. v. Johnson, 891 S.W.2d 640, 10 IER Cases 427 (Tex. 1995).

[12] Pierce v. Commonwealth Life Ins. Co., 40 F.3d 796, 806 (6th Cir. 1994).

[13] 903 P.2d 888 (Or. App. 1995), *review allowed,* 909 P.2d 161 (Or. 1996).

of any physical constraint, but only the threat of potential loss of employment, does not work a false imprisonment.[14]

## B. Surveillance

On remand from the Ohio Court of Appeals, the Ohio Court of Claims awarded damages for the surveillance of an employee restroom.[15]

## D. Search

### *2. Private Sector: Privacy*

*a. Credit Records.* In *Pulla v. Amoco Oil Co.,*[16] an employee, disgruntled over a coworker's abuse of sick leave, pulled up the coworker's personal credit card use and compared the dates of purchases against the dates he had called in sick. She reported the discrepancies to management which, while admonishing her against having done so, proceeded itself to that comparison. In sustaining the jury's award of damages for invasion of privacy, the trial court rejected the claim that a legitimate objective is a complete defense to an invasion of privacy or that an employer has a legitimate interest in reviewing an employee's confidential records:

> [T]he court reads these cases as standing for the more narrow proposition that the employer's interest must be balanced against the degree of intrusion resulting from the employer's methods to obtain the information in question. The court concludes here, as a reasonable jury could have, that whatever Amoco's interest may have been, its methods were unduly intrusive when balanced against that interest. Amoco used confidential credit card records for a purpose for which they were never intended, and did so surreptitiously, without notice to, or consent or knowledge of, the credit card holder.[17]

*b. Automobiles.* In *Terrell v. Rowsey,*[18] a supervisor who had earlier entered an employee's unlocked car in the company parking lot and found a quantity of beer, and who suspected the employee of drinking beer on

[14]Randall's Food Mkts., Inc. v. Johnson, 891 S.W.2d 640 (Tex. 1995); Trahan v. Bellsouth Telecommunications, Inc., 881 F. Supp. 1080 (W.D. La. 1995).

[15]Speer v. Department of Rehabilitation & Correction, 646 N.E.2d 273 (Ohio Ct. Cl. 1994). *Cf.* Gilbert v. Sears, Roebuck & Co., 899 F. Supp. 597 (M.D. Fla. 1995) (on surveillance of customer in men's room). In Molt v. Lindsay Mfg. Co., 532 N.W.2d 11 (Neb. 1995), an employee was dismissed for pilfering from a change machine after he had been video recorded by a camera secreted for that purpose. No objection to the offering of the tape was made at trial (thus failing to preserve that issue for appeal), nor was any challenge made to the use of the video camera for that surveillance purpose.

[16]882 F. Supp. 836 (S.D. Iowa 1994), *aff'd in part and rev'd in part,* 72 F.3d 648 (8th Cir. 1995).

[17]*Id.* at 867 (footnote omitted).

[18]647 N.E.2d 662, 10 IER Cases 650 (Ind. Ct. App. 1995).

the premises—that is, in his car—in violation of company policy, opened the car door while the employee was sitting in it and seized an opened bottle of beer secreted under a blanket. The trial court's grant of summary judgment for the company on the employee's suit for invasion of privacy was sustained. The majority opined:

> Terrell [the employee] had no absolute right to be free from an invasion of privacy, but rather a right to be free from unreasonable invasions of privacy. The trial court held that the intrusion was not unreasonable in light of the following: Terrell's diminished privacy interest while on Red Giant's [the employer] property, Red Giant's rule against drinking on company property, which includes the right to require chemical screening tests, Red Giant's obligation to provide employees a safe work place, and the momentary entrance of Terrell's car with no physical contact with Terrell. We agree with the trial court that, as a matter of law, Rowsey's actions do not offend a person of ordinary sensibility. Terrell was on his employer's property and he admitted to drinking alcohol, despite Red Giant's policy against drinking. Furthermore, Rowsey acted out of responsibility for the safety of Terrell and his fellow employees and the intrusion was minimal.[19]

The dissenting judge surveyed the law on point rather more thoroughly and opined:

> The employer was clearly entitled to prohibit consumption or possession of alcohol by employees on the premises and to discipline employees who are under the influence in the work place. That entitlement, however, does not include the prying into private places in which an employee has every expectation of privacy. Such a place is one's private vehicle, whether parked on the employer's property or otherwise. Most reasonable persons would have a belief and expectation that their private vehicle will not be entered and searched by unauthorized individuals.[20]

He would hold it a legitimate question of fact whether the search was or was not reasonable; that is, a jury might well find the intrusion, even if seemingly minimal, nevertheless "wrongful and offensive."[21]

*c. Mail.* In *Doe v. Kohn Nast & Graf, P.C.*,[22] the plaintiff alleged that his employer, a law firm, opened his mail—some of it marked "personal"—and that this act worked an invasion of privacy. The court held that an employer is not authorized to open mail directed to a person at the workplace "that appears to be personal"[23] and held it to be a jury question whether or not the employer reasonably believed that it was authorized to open the employee's mail. The court further held it to be

---

[19]*Id.* at 667.
[20]*Id.*
[21]*Id.* at 669.
[22]866 F. Supp. 190 (E.D. Pa. 1994).
[23]*Id.* at 195–96.

a jury question whether the firm processed the mail "in a manner calculated to protect" the employee's privacy:

> The method by which an employer carries out an authorized inquiry into an employee's private concerns may constitute an intrusion upon the employee's seclusion if that method fails to give due regard to the employee's privacy or reveals personal matters unrelated to the workplace. . . .
>
> . . . In this case, even if defendants reasonably believed that the letters to plaintiff from media outlets were related to firm business, the defendants might still have invaded plaintiff's privacy by retaining copies of the letters, once they had determined that the letters were personal, and sending them on to plaintiff without informing him that the letters had been opened.
>
> The defendants also argue that a reasonable person would not have found the acts alleged to be "highly offensive." The alleged acts described above create a genuine issue of material fact as to this issue.[24]

*d. Desks and Credenzas.* In an earlier decision, *Doe v. Kohn Nast & Graf, P.C.,*[25] the employee complained as well of a search of personal documents left on his desk. The court held that such an act could be actionable only if it was "certain" that the individual inspecting or searching lacked the necessary legal or personal permission to do so, and if the intrusion was "substantial" and highly offensive to a reasonable person.[26] (These all were held to present jury questions.) That reasoning was followed in *O'Bryan v. KTIV Television*[27] concerning an alleged search of a salesperson's desk and credenza for sales records. The desk was not locked and was kept in an open sales area among other salespeoples' desks. The court held that the plaintiff lacked a reasonable expectation that his desk would not be searched for company documents, especially in view of the salesperson's assumption that fellow salespeople would have to resort to his desk to retrieve employment-related documents.

The U.S. Court of Appeals for the Eighth Circuit held that inasmuch as North Dakota had not extended its common law of privacy to an intrusion into one's seclusion or solitude, the court would recognize no cause of action for a supervisor's opening of an employee's locked desk in order to obtain his personnel file.[28]

*e. Frisk.* An employer is not liable for the frisking of a potentially violent employee by a police officer who was asked to be present when

---

[24]*Id.* at 196.

[25]862 F. Supp. 1310 (E.D. Pa. 1994).

[26]*Id.* at 1376.

[27]868 F. Supp. 1146 (N.D. Iowa 1994), *aff'd in part and rev'd in part*, 64 F.3d 1188 (8th Cir. 1995).

[28]Nelson v. J.C. Penny Co., 70 F.3d 962 (8th Cir. 1995), *vacated in part*, 75 F.3d 343 (8th Cir. 1996).

the employee was to be given notice of discharge, absent evidence that the employer participated in the frisk or that the police were acting as the employer's agent.[29]

## III. MONITORING THE WORKPLACE

### A. Electronic Interception and Nonelectronic Eavesdropping[30]

#### *1. Telephonic Interception: Federal Regulation*

The ability of a public employer to intercept the telephone conversation of its employees is governed by the Fourth Amendment. One court has held that analysis of this amendment imports a two-pronged test:

> whether the individual exhibited a subjective expectation of privacy, and whether that expectation is one which society is prepared to recognize as reasonable. . . . The determination of reasonableness requires a balancing of the need for the search against the severity of the invasion of personal rights, and courts must weigh "the scope of the particular intrusion, the manner in which it is conducted, the justification for initiating it, and the place in which it is conducted."[31]

In this case, the state police had installed telephone monitoring systems in several of its facilities in which phones were used by state troopers (as well as by arrestees and lawyers), but not all telephones were monitored; some indicated monitoring (by a recurrent beep) even when they were not monitored, and others lacked any such indication even when they were being monitored. The court held that the reasonableness of the troopers' expectation of privacy depended on the absence of notice that the telephones were being monitored and so presented a fact question for the jury.

Another court put the Fourth Amendment analysis somewhat differently but to the same effect: the test is whether a person had a "legitimate expectation of privacy" and, if so, whether the person's privacy interest outweighed the public need for the interception.[32] In this case, the court held that city dispatchers had no reasonable expectation that their private telephone conversations would not be recorded when they were aware

---

[29]Koepplin v. Zortman Mining, Inc., 881 P.2d 1306, 9 IER Cases 1636 (Mont. 1994). To the same effect, see Raines v. Shoney's, Inc., 909 F. Supp. 1070 (E.D. Tenn. 1995) (search conducted by police summoned by employer).

[30]*See generally* Note, *Privacy Issues in the Private-Sector Workplace: Protection From Electronic Surveillance and the Emerging "Privacy Gap,"* 67 S. CAL. L. REV. 441 (1994).

[31]In re State Police Litig., 888 F. Supp. 1235, 1255 (D. Conn. 1995) (references omitted).

[32]Hart v. Clearfield City, 815 F. Supp. 1544, 10 IER Cases 1623 (D. Utah 1993).

of the extensive monitoring that took place, despite the fact that they believed on the basis of prior malfunction that a particular line was not then being monitored. So, too, in *Griffin v. City of Milwaukee,*[33] the openness of the monitoring conducted by the city's police dispatching office was held to amount to consent as a matter of law: dispatchers (including the plaintiff) were told that calls might be monitored and that incoming emergency calls would be recorded, and the recording equipment was in a glass case in the middle of the plaintiff's work area.

### *3. Telephonic Interception: State Law*

State law may track the federal Electronic Communications Privacy Act[34] in allowing an exception for an interception by a telephone subscriber "in the ordinary course of its business," as does the law of Connecticut. Applying that language, a federal district court held that the monitoring of state troopers' *outgoing* private telephone calls could not be shown to have any relationship to the department's need to monitor, which concerned only incoming communications, and so could not be in the ordinary course of business.[35] Monitoring of incoming calls is often conducted by customer service departments of commercial enterprises.[36]

### *4. Interception of Oral Communication: State Law*

Illinois law makes it an offense in the civil setting to use an "eavesdropping device to hear or record all or any part of a conversation" without the consent of *all* parties to the conversation.[37] An "eavesdropping device" is defined as

> any device capable of being used to hear or record oral conversation whether such conversation is conducted in person, by telephone, or by any other means; Provided, however, that this definition shall not include devices used for the restoration of the deaf or hard-of-hearing to normal or partial hearing.[38]

The statute is subject to several exemptions, to which the Illinois legislature added the following in 1995:

---

[33] 74 F.3d 824, 11 IER Cases 560 (7th Cir. 1996).

[34] 18 U.S.C. §§2510–21 (1993).

[35] In re State Police Litig., 888 F. Supp. 1235 (D. Conn. 1995).

[36] In one such case, the monitor overheard one customer agent importune another for homosexual sex while transferring a call (the customer was on hold at the time). The employee was discharged and his unemployment compensation denied on the basis of the monitor's testimony, there being apparently no objection to the monitoring. Tuttle v. Mellon Bank, 659 A.2d 786 (Del. Super. Ct. 1995).

[37] ILL. COMP. STAT. ANN., ch. 720, §5/14-2 (1993).

[38] *Id.*

> The use of a monitoring system by any corporation or other business entity engaged in the provision of products or services to the public, or to the officers, employees, or agents thereof, when the acts otherwise prohibited herein are for the purpose of service quality control or for educational, training, or research purposes and such acts are performed with the consent of one party to the communication being intercepted.[39]

After litigation challenging the sweep of the law—which allowed any employer to monitor for "educational, training, or research purposes"—the law was narrowed considerably the following year.[40] It now allows:

> The use of a telephone monitoring device by either (1) a corporation or other business entity engaged in marketing or opinion research or (2) a corporation or other business entity engaged in telephone solicitation, as defined in this subsection, to record or listen to oral telephone solicitation conversations or marketing or opinion research conversations by an employee of the corporation or other business entity when:
>
> (I) The monitoring is used for the purpose of service quality control of marketing or opinion research or telephone solicitation, the education or training of employees or contractors engaged in marketing or opinion research or telephone solicitation, or internal research related to marketing or opinion research or telephone solicitation; and
>
> (II) The monitoring is used with the consent of at least one person who is an active party to the marketing or opinion research conversation or telephone solicitation conversation being monitored.

The law requires notice to employees that monitoring or recording may occur, including the prominent posting of signs; requires employers to terminate listening or recording as soon as practicable upon learning that a conversation does not relate to marketing or opinion research or telephone solicitation; and requires employers to provide employee access to telephones that are not subject to monitoring or recording (e.g., pay telephones). "Telephone solicitation" and "marketing or opinion research" is subject to express statutory definition.

The use of a tape recorder by an employer to record conversations with supervisors or management was considered by the National Labor Relations Board; it sustained without comment the conclusion of the Board's Administrative Law Judge that a discharge for a refusal to turn off and remove the recording device provided a valid ground for discharge.[41] Likewise, a federal district court held that the secret taping of a supervisor during a performance evaluation supplied a valid ground for discharge.[42]

---

[39] *Id.* §5/14-3(j), Illinois Laws of 1995, Pub. Act 89-14-3.

[40] PL 89-452, 1996 Ill. Laws 452.

[41] Dana Corp., 318 NLRB No. 30 (1995).

[42] Hashop v. Rockwell Space Operations Co., 867 F. Supp. 1287 (S.D. Tex. 1994).

## B. Computer Communications and Electronic Mail

Additional literature is noted below.[43]

# IV. DISCLOSURE OF EVALUATIONS AND INVESTIGATIONS

## A. Defamation

It is generally recognized that a nonverbal act can make a statement that is actionable in defamation, e.g., taking an employee for interrogation from a medical office waiting room three times in the view of his coworkers in connection with a bomb threat[44] or leading an employee through the store in handcuffs.[45] On the other hand, no defamation was worked by a superior who asked an employee in the presence of others to clear out his desk, return his keys, and leave the premises; escorted the employee to the elevator; requested his building pass while in the presence of others in the elevator; and, at the exit and again in the presence of others, had the employee's personal belongings inspected.[46]

The Supreme Court of Minnesota has refused to find defamatory a superior's accompanying a discharged employee to the employee's office, remaining while he packed his belongings, and escorting him to the door in full view of coworkers.[47] Reviewing the law in other jurisdictions, the court noted that conduct was held actionable where it rose to the level of a "dramatic pantomine," a clearly discernable interplay of words and conduct.[48] The instant case involved no spoken word *or* defamatory conduct other than an escort to the door in which the employer's agent intentionally walked behind the discharged employee to avoid drawing attention.

### *1. Publication*

According to the U.S. Court of Appeals for the Tenth Circuit, Oklahoma would still adhere to its rule that an intracorporate communication is not "published," and so internal communications made in the process

---

[43]Lee, *Watch Your E-Mail! Employee E-Mail Monitoring and Privacy Law in the Age of the "Electronic Sweatshop,"* 28 J. MARSHALL L. REV. 139 (1994); Comment, *E-Mail and Voice Mail: Employee Privacy and the Federal Wiretap Statute,* 44 AM. U. L. REV. 219 (1994).

[44]Hall v. Hercules, Inc., 494 F.2d 420 (10th Cir. 1974).

[45]Caldor, Inc. v. Bowden, 625 A.2d 959 (Md. 1993).

[46]Dubrovin v. Marshall Field's & Co. Employee's Credit Union, 536 N.E.2d 800 (Ill. App. Ct. 1989).

[47]Bolton v. Department of Human Servs., 540 N.W.2d 523, 11 IER Cases 369 (Minn. 1995).

[48]540 N.W.2d at 525.

of an employer's investigation would not be subject to any action for defamation.[49] And an intermediate appellate court in Illinois ruminated in passing on whether such should be the law in that jurisdiction:

> [I]s a statement by the person in authority to another person involved in the investigation a publication. Unquestionably, a statement accusing plaintiff of attempted theft by the assistant manager to a person not involved in the investigation of the alleged theft would be a publication of such. In this case, however, the statement by [the assistant store manager] was made to plaintiff in the presence of her supervisor, the person who initiated the investigation. Is the law such that a member of an investigatory team cannot give his or her opinion to another member of the team as to the guilt of a suspect without creating an actionable cause for defamation?[50]

But the court declined the invitation to address the question in view of the parties' agreement that the statements made were conditionally privileged.

The Connecticut Supreme Court has noted that the idea that an intracorporate communication is not "published" for defamation purposes has been almost completely abandoned.[51] That court refused to adopt this idea.

*2. Consent*

In *Hooper v. Pitney Bowes, Inc.*,[52] the company's management received complaints that a highly successful sales manager was conducting emotionally charged (and, to the complainants, objectionable) motivational sales meetings that those in attendance characterized as "cult-like."[53] Two managers commenced an investigation that included off-premises meetings; secret recordings; library research on the occult; and private meetings with employees during which one manager made statements characterizing the manager under investigation as "cultist," a "sorceress," "satanistic," and a "witch."[54] The jury's finding that one of the manager's statements—otherwise slanderous and uttered with "malice" (i.e., unprivileged)—was consented to was sustained on appeal:

> There is testimony from several sources that [the plaintiff] never denied the accusations against her when she was confronted with them; that she actually claimed she was engaged in "cult-like" activities; that she asked her supervisors to investigate her activities so the allegations of cultism could be "cleared up";

---

[49]Starr v. Pearle Vision, Inc., 54 F.3d 1548 (10th Cir. 1995).

[50]Harrel v. Dillards Dep't Stores, 644 N.E.2d 448, 452 (Ill. App. Ct. 1994).

[51]Torosyan v. Boehringer Ingelheim Pharmaceuticals, Inc., 662 A.2d 89, 103, 10 IER Cases 1313 (Conn. 1995).

[52]895 S.W.2d 773 (Tex. Ct. App. 1995).

[53]*Id.* at 776.

[54]*Id.*

> that she told the managers that she knew her actions could reasonably be considered as cultish . . .[55]

### 3. *Privilege*

*a. Disregard of Truth: The Duty to Investigate.* In *Bell v. Evening Post Publishing Co.*,[56] the trial court's grant of summary judgment for the company was affirmed in an opinion that succinctly outlined how a privilege attaches to a thorough and professionally conducted investigation. Bell was a zone manager for the newspaper. Bell's assistant (with whom he had had an affair) reported to management that Bell was sexually harassing her; she also reported that Bell was currently having an affair with another employee. Two of the company's management officials interviewed that employee at her home, asking her if she knew anything of the allegations against Bell; they did not inform her of Bell's prior affair with his assistant. Thereafter, they met with Bell to allow him to respond. Bell was discharged.

The court held that a qualified privilege attached to the investigation and that this privilege had not been exceeded: the only utterance of defamatory remarks outside the circle of the investigation was made to the employee who was interviewed at her home. The officials merely asked her

> whether she had any knowledge of the truth or falsity of the sexual harassment allegations against Bell. These questions were properly limited in scope to determine whether sexual harassment was occurring in the Evening Post workplace and were properly directed at protecting Evening Post's interest in preventing sexual harassment by its supervisory personnel.[57]

Moreover, the location of that interview was calculated to *avoid* the suspicion of other workers.

The Illinois Appellate Court supplied a fuller exposition, under what it took to be a higher standard announced by that state's highest court, that a plaintiff must show

> either a direct intention to injure another, as opposed to merely proving defendant knew the matter was false, or a reckless disregard of the defamee's rights and of the consequences that may result to her, as opposed to merely proving that defendant had a high degree of knowledge that the matter was false.[58]

The plaintiff was a salesperson who had put store items—some purchased by her, some that she alleged she was holding for later purchase—in a

---

[55] *Id.* at 778.

[56] 459 S.E.2d 315 (S.C. Ct. App. 1995).

[57] *Id.* at 317.

[58] Harrel v. Dillards Dep't Stores, 644 N.E.2d 448, 452 (Ill. App. Ct. 1994), citing Kuwik v. Starmark Star Mktg. & Admin., 619 N.E.2d 129 (Ill. 1993).

bag in a stockroom. The bag was found and the incident investigated by two store mangers who interviewed other clerks and security personnel. After the managers interviewed her, they rechecked her account with others whom she had indicated. She was informed in a meeting in the presence of her immediate supervisor that she was being discharged for intending to steal the two items she had not paid for. The appellate court found the evidence to have required a verdict for the company, in part because of the standard governing the adequacy of employer investigations:

> The issue is whether the investigation by the defendant was so deficient that it was apparent that [the manager] had a high degree of awareness that his conclusion that plaintiff was attempting to steal the items was false, or that he entertained such serious doubts as to the truth of concluding that plaintiff was attempting to steal the merchandise that he recklessly disregarded plaintiff's rights and the consequences that might result to her. . . .
>
> . . . .
>
> Plaintiff does not suggest where or how there was a deficiency in the manner of the investigation. Plaintiff does not contend that there were other witnesses that should have been interviewed or that somehow defendant had the ability to obtain or should have obtained any physical evidence. . . .
>
> Plaintiff hints that there should have been eyewitness evidence for the discharge to be justified. The lack of eyewitness information cannot serve as the basis for an improper investigation, as circumstantial evidence is often the most compelling and reliable evidence available. . . .
>
> Plaintiff does not deny that the circumstances were suspicious and that her act of using a fictitious name to hold items was a violation of company rules, that a similar circumstance for which she was given a warning had occurred before, and that her offer to resign could have been misconstrued as an admission of guilt.[59]

The court also ruled in part on policy grounds:

> Finally, there can be little question that a finding of liability in this case would be a notice to all employers not to tell employees why they are being fired. Nor would a cautious employer even conduct an investigation for fear that someone might make a defamatory statement. The cautious employer would either fire an at-will employee immediately upon receiving notice of some problem or else keep the employee in spite of reservations as to the honesty of such employee and the example it would set for other employees. Causing unnecessary fear of litigation is a needless burden on our society.[60]

The result, however, would not appear to be different under the prevailing view in most jurisdictions of what constitutes "malice" (i.e., a reckless disregard of truth).[61] Suffice it to say that an investigation that fails to pursue evidence that refutes an allegation of misconduct may be

---

[59] *Id.* at 454.

[60] *Id.*

[61] *See, e.g.*, Hagler v. Proctor & Gamble Mfg. Co., 884 S.W.2d 771 (Tex. 1994).

taken as evidence of such disregard for the truth as to defeat a privilege,[62] but investigators need not accept an employee's offer to submit to a polygraph.[63]

*b. Disclosure Within the Firm.* Allegations of incompetence or wrongdoing made within the circle of those with a legitimate need for or interest in the information are privileged if the dissemination is not more broad than the interest justifies. Such a privilege extends to communications from a medical school department chair to the school's dean concerning possible misconduct by a member of the department,[64] to observations on a medical department chair's fitness for office made to medical meetings of the hospital reviewing the chair's performance (and to which he had an opportunity to respond),[65] and to a report to a manager of possible employee drug use that the manager reported in turn to others in the managerial hierarchy with responsibility for the matter of employee drug use.[66]

A recurring vexing issue is the report of an employee's discharge to coworkers or to a broader circle of supervisory or other employees in order to quash rumors, to allay suspicion of arbitrariness or wrongful action, or to emphasize the fact that the employer takes its rules seriously and enforces them. Some jurisdictions give considerable weight to these interests. In *Castleberry v. Boeing Co.*,[67] a manager was discharged for having condoned an office party for a coworker where a "gag" gift of a dildo was presented. (The fact that there had recently been a program emphasizing the importance the company attached to preventing sexual harassment weighed heavily in the decision, even though the party's guest of honor did not object to the gift.) The fact of the discharge and the reason for it was reported in a meeting of more than 250 other managers. Nevertheless, the scope of disclosure was held privileged inasmuch as they all were considered to have an interest in the matter.

Similarly, in *Posyniak v. School Sisters of St. Francis of St. Joseph's Covenant*,[68] the interim management of a nursing home informed the staff of its longtime executive director's resignation in a way that implied laxity in his performance. The court held the dissemination privileged,

---

[62]Torosyan v. Boehringer Ingelheim Pharmaceuticals, Inc., 662 A.2d 89, 10 IER Cases 1313 (Conn. 1995).

[63]Molt v. Linsay Mfg. Co., 532 N.W.2d 11 (Neb. 1995).

[64]El Deeb v. University of Minn., 60 F.3d 423 (8th Cir. 1995).

[65]Muthuswamy v. Burke, 646 N.E.2d 616 (Ill. App. Ct. 1993).

[66]Thomas v. St. Luke's Health Sys., Inc. 869 F. Supp. 1413 (N.D. Iowa 1994), *aff'd*, 61 F.3d 908 (8th Cir. 1995).

[67]880 F. Supp. 1435 (D. Kan. 1995).

[68]511 N.W.2d 300 (Wis. Ct. App. 1993).

stating that the nursing home "had a legitimate interest in maintaining morale and quieting rumors regarding Posyniak's status."[69]

In *Schrader v. Eli Lilly & Co.*,[70] the employer dismissed several senior employees who were suspected of theft. The circumstances were explained in a slide presentation to a staff managerial meeting. One manager posted the notes of the meeting, thus making them accessible to the plant's 1500 workers. The Indiana Supreme Court held the posting to have been privileged:

> The posted notes were a communication from the employer to employees concerning a matter that affected both. Each had common interests in the communication: job performance and job security. The reason for the communication was to preserve those interests. When Lilly management initially addressed the warehouse situation, they acted not only to inform those individuals immediately affected by the discharges—the former employees department heads and supervisors—but also to suppress rumors and speculation running throughout the Lilly Tippecanoe County complex, as well as to communicate the core values of Eli Lilly and Company. The rumors had an adverse impact on employee productivity and morale throughout the complex. There was testimony in the trial court that the rumors were widespread and pervasive throughout the entire complex. Lilly management acted to stop the rumors by issuing the statements.[71]

The Wisconsin Court of Appeals put the issue even point pointedly: In this court's opinion, an employer is privileged to communicate to its entire workforce the reasons for a discharge "with impunity."[72]

Other jurisdictions give greater weight to the reputational (or dignitary) harm resulting from so wide a dissemination. Thus, the claim that managers told a number of coworkers "far beyond the small circle of executives" of an employee's alleged wrongdoing was sufficient to withstand a motion to dismiss on grounds of privilege,[73] a complaint by a dismissed academic department chair regarding a letter to the faculty explaining that action withstood a motion for summary judgment,[74] and an allegation that a manager told nonmanagerial employees that a coworker had been dismissed for misappropriating funds also survived a motion for summary judgment.[75] In the latter case, the company had a policy assuring confidentiality in personnel matters. Further, the statement regarding the dismissed employee

---

[69] *Id.* at 305.

[70] 639 N.E.2d 258, 9 IER Cases 1830 (Ind. 1994) (the lower court decision is discussed in the main text at p. 131).

[71] *Id.* at 263.

[72] Olson v. 3M Co., 523 N.W.2d 578, 585 (Wis. Ct. App. 1994).

[73] Masso v. United Parcel Serv. of Am., Inc., 884 F. Supp. 610 (D. Mass. 1995).

[74] Kovacs v. Briarcliffe School, Inc., 617 N.Y.S.2d 804 (App. Div. 1994).

[75] Schrimsher v. Liberty Nat'l Life Ins. Co., 655 So. 2d 986, 10 IER Cases 798 (Ala. 1995).

> could not have had any bearing on the other agents' duties or responsibilities. . . . There was no evidence that the other agents, who were merely co-workers with Schrimsher, had any interest corresponding to the interest the management of Liberty National had in the reason for Schrimsher's termination.[76]

*c. Disclosure Outside the Firm.* Reports made to governmental agencies with an interest in the matter are privileged—sometimes absolutely.[77] But statements made to others outside the firm, especially to customers or clients, about the employee's departure may be actionable depending on the need for or purpose of the communication.[78] Thus, a bank executive is privileged to communicate to the bank's shareholders the reasons for significant losses even when they are attributable to a former executive's performance.[79]

A recurring—and vexing—issue concerns the issuance of press releases or other public statements. The issue was confronted in *Olson v. 3M Co.*,[80] in which an employee's complaint of sexual harassment, made both to the local police and to the company, resulted in the discharge of two employees. The company issued a press release regarding the discharge that was picked up in the local media. The company's statement provided in pertinent part:

> An investigation by 3M into allegations of harassment at its Prairie du Chien, Wisconsin, plant resulted in the termination of two production employees and the resignation of two production employees Thursday. The Company launched the investigation last December immediately after it was notified of the alleged activities.
>
> "Our position is very clear: incidents of this nature simply are not tolerated at 3M facilities," said Prairie du Chien plant manager Maynard Schultz.
>
> Schultz added that all employees at Prairie du Chien had received training about 3M's policy prohibiting harassment of any type.
>
> Details of the circumstances leading to the terminations and resignations were not disclosed.[81]

The court held the release qualifiedly privileged on the ground that it furthered a common interest:

> It is undisputed that many in the Prairie du Chien community knew of the harassment investigation. 3M had an important interest in letting the community know that it took seriously its obligation to provide a harassment-free workplace. Communication to the community on the results of the investigation

---

[76] *Id.* at 988 (footnote omitted).

[77] *See, e.g.*, Davis v. Copelan, 452 S.E.2d 194 (Ga. Ct. App. 1994) (report to state Department of Labor absolutely privileged); McBride v. Pizza Hut, Inc., 658 A.2d 205 (D.C. App. 1995) (same).

[78] *See, e.g.*, Kelleher v. Corinthian Media, Inc., 617 N.Y.S.2d 726 (App. Div. 1994).

[79] Young v. First United Bank, 516 N.W.2d 256 (Neb. 1994).

[80] 523 N.W.2d 578 (Wis. Ct. App. 1994).

[81] *Id.* at 581.

> and the actions 3M had taken served to protect that interest. We conclude that a conditional privilege attaches to 3M's communications to the community.[82]

It has also been said that charitable institutions have a qualified privilege to communicate with contributors, employees, and others involved in their activities regarding allegations of employee wrongdoing. That privilege has been extended not only to major figures, such as the chief financial officer of United Way,[83] but also to employees in a university's facilities department.[84] The same has been said of figures who are employed in publicly visible positions in the media: neither a self-serving statement of why a television reporter was terminated nor a public apology for a talk radio host's remarks was actionable respectively for emotional distress[85] or defamation.[86] Further, a corporation is not obligated to confirm or deny in the press allegations of wrongdoing made by a third party.[87]

### B. Privacy

#### *1. Intrusion*

In *Simon v. Moorehouse School of Medicine,*[88] a federal district court, applying Georgia law, affirmed the conclusion of a U.S. magistrate that the rape of an employee by her superior (with whom she had had an affair) worked an "unreasonable intrusion upon . . . [her] seclusion" and so was actionable as a tort.[89]

#### *2. Disclosure of Facts*

The major lines of inquiry are whether the facts were disclosed so widely as to constitute an intrusion and whether they were of so private a nature as to work an injury.

*a. Scope of Disclosure.* The courts continue to be vexed about how widespread a disclosure is required actionably to invade one's privacy.

---

[82]*Id.* at 586.

[83]Merlo v. United Way of Am., 43 F.3d 96 (4th Cir. 1994).

[84]Gallo v. Princeton Univ., 656 A.2d 1267, 10 IER Cases 889 (N.J. Super. Ct. App. Div. 1995).

[85]Phillips v. Pacific & S. Co., 451 S.E.2d 100 (Ga. Ct. App. 1994).

[86]Calton v. CV Radio Assoc., 639 N.E.2d 1249, 10 IER Cases 1116 (Ohio Ct. App. 1994).

[87]Tischmann v. ITT/Sheraton Corp., 882 F. Supp. 1358 (S.D.N.Y. 1995).

[88]908 F. Supp. 959 (N.D. Ga. 1995). In Frederick v. Reed Smith Shaw & McClay, 1994 WL 57213 (E.D. Pa. 1994), a partner in a law firm responded to press questions by imputing criminal and psychological problems to the plaintiff, a former associate. The court held the statements defamatory; privilege was not apparently raised.

[89]908 F. Supp. at 973.

In *Blackthorne v. Posner,*[90] an employee complained that his employer had "disclosed private medical and family matters to third persons," but the court held that that was inadequate because the tort required disclosure to "the public or to a large number of persons."[91] So, too, in *Doe v. Methodist Hospital,*[92] the disclosure by Doe's coworker's wife (a nurse in a hospital) to her husband that Doe had tested positive for HIV was held too limited to be actionable, but that holding provoked the following dissent:

> It is true that many jurisdictions require disclosure to the public at large, not just a few people, in order to state an actionable claim for this type of invasion of privacy. However, other jurisdictions follow the rule that where (1) a plaintiff is not a public figure and (2) he has a special relationship with the "public" to whom the private fact is disclosed, the publicity requirement may be satisfied by disclosure to a particular public such as fellow employees, club members, church members and neighbors. *See Beaumont v. Brown* (1977), 401 Mich. 80, 257 N.W.2d 522, 531; *Miller v. Motorola, Inc.* (1990), 202 Ill. App. 3d 976, 148 Ill. Dec. 303, 306, 560 N.E.2d 900, 903; *see also McSurely v. McClellan* (D.C. Cir. 1985), 753 F.2d 88, 112, *cert. denied*, 474 U.S. 1005, 106 S. Ct. 525, 88 L.Ed.2d 457. Communication to the general public is not required because disclosure to those persons with whom the plaintiff has a special relationship may be just as devastating as disclosure to many.[93]

Where the disclosure is made to a small group but wider dissemination of the information is naturally to be assumed as a consequence, the publication requirement may be satisfied. In *Arroyo v. Rosen,*[94] for example, a medical researcher who had complained of another researcher's scientific fraud gave the first page of a report of a Committee of Inquiry to a reporter even though the report was confidential. The release was held actionable.

Just as in the law of defamation,[95] the public disclosure of private facts may be conditionally privileged, and the same question of the scope of the privilege vis-a-vis disclosure to coworkers may be posed here. For example, in *Smith v. Arkansas Louisiana Gas Co.,*[96] management disclosed in a meeting of 30 to 35 field and service workers that the plaintiff, the manager of the service department, had been demoted because of engaging in sexual harassment. The court held the statement to be privileged.[97]

---

[90]883 F. Supp. 1443 (D. Or. 1995).

[91]To the same effect, see Freeman v. Unisys Corp., 870 F. Supp. 169 (E.D. Mich. 1994).

[92]639 N.E.2d 683 (Ind. Ct. App. 1994).

[93]*Id.* at 686 (Najam, J., dissenting).

[94]648 A.2d 1074 (Md. 1994).

[95]*See supra* §IV.A.

[96]645 So. 2d 785 (La. Ct. App. 1994).

[97]In Kersey v. United Shoe Corp., 440 S.E.2d 250 (Ga. Ct. App. 1994), the employee's admitted complicity in cheating—her admission of the truth of the charge—negated her suit for libel against the company for having circulated that fact as the ground of discharge. But

*b. Private Facts.* Some facts may be so public that disclosure—or further disclosure—works no invasion of privacy. Such was the holding in *Merlo v. United Way of America*[98] concerning the public release of a report prepared for United Way's governing board regarding the plaintiff's management as Chief Financial Officer in the wake of a public scandal. Essentially, the plaintiff, having been thrust into the public light as a participant in a newsworthy event, lost any claim that the facts reported were "private."[99] On the other hand, some facts, though private, are not of such a nature—so intimate or personal—as to give rise to a tort if disclosed. So, for example, where a restaurant manager circulated a birthday card among coworkers to be presented to a waitress that included a reference to her age, 68, the court held the disclosure inactionable.[100]

*3. False Light*

An action in "false light" has been held subject to the same requirements of publicity (and privilege) as have other theories of privacy.[101] And inasmuch as New York does not recognize any nonstatutory right to privacy, that nonrecognition extends to claims asserted under this head as well.[102]

---

the plaintiff did not pursue and so the court did not address the question of privacy posed by the disclosure.

[98]43 F.3d 96 (4th Cir. 1994).

[99]*See also* Keenan v. Allan, 889 F. Supp. 1320 (E.D. Wash. 1995) (on "false light" grounds—no cause of action where the matter was of fair public comment).

[100]Galdauckas v. Interstate Hotels Corp. No. 16, 901 F. Supp. 454 (D. Mass. 1995).

[101]Zielinski v. Clorox Co., 450 S.E.2d 222 (Ga. Ct. App. 1994); Freeman v. Unysis Corp., 870 F. Supp. 169 (E.D. Mich. 1994); Arroyo v. Rosen, 648 A.2d 1074 (Md. 1994).

[102]Cardone v. Empire Blue Cross & Blue Shield, 884 F. Supp. 838 (S.D.N.Y. 1995).

CHAPTER 6

# CONTROL OF EMPLOYEES

## I. ASSOCIATION AND EXPRESSION

The extent to which expression and association are protected in the context of at-will employment—absent some explicit statutory violation—was considered by the Supreme Court of Nevada in *Bigelow v. Bullard.*[1] Michael Bullard and Ricky Hammer worked for Bigelow Holding Company, apparently a residential apartment ownership or management company with a long-standing practice of racial discrimination. When three black males came on the property, a coworker of Bullard radioed that fact to a managerial or supervising employee, Donna Dallman. Bullard told the coworker that "blacks had rights, too," and the coworker apparently reported this remark to Dallman when she arrived. This report, according to Bullard's testimony, resulted in the following:

> Donna walks up to where I'm sitting, picks up the piece of paper that I'm writing on, and she said, "what's your fucking problem?"
>
> I said, "I don't have a problem."
>
> She said, "I think you do." She said, "I think you're a fucking nigger lover. Sit your God damn ass down on that fucking stool, shut your mouth, and do your fucking work."
>
> Q. What happened next?
>
> A. Then she said, "On second thought, get your fucking ass out of here. I don't want you working for me anymore."
>
> Q. And what was the time span between those two statements by Mrs. Dallman [sic]?
>
> A. Not even 30 seconds.[2]

Hammer was also discharged based on her friendship with Bullard (they apparently shared an apartment).

The jury's verdict for Hammer and Bullard on grounds of a discharge violative of public policy was reversed. The court stressed that Bullard had not been discharged for refusing to do an unlawful act or for protesting to management any arguable wrong it was committing. Accepting his facts as true (as the jury had), the only inference to be drawn is that

---

[1]901 P.2d 630, 10 IER Cases 1635 (Nev. 1995).

[2]901 P.2d at 632 n.3.

Bullard was dismissed because of what management thought an "overly sympathetic attitude toward African-Americans."[3] It was not a rebellious statement or a protestation, and "could not be described in any sense as being insubordinate or 'disloyal.' "[4]

> In sum, then, we do not deem it to be consistent with the employment law of this state to hold that an employee's merely expressing to a fellow employee or some third person disapproval of or "objection" to company policy that is claimed to be contrary to public policy (as distinguished from refusal to carry out that policy) can be the predicate for a tortious discharge action. Dallman fired Bullard not for what he *did* (such as refusing to carry out ugly and unlawful racist policies for the company or even for "objecting" to such policies) but rather, at worst, for what, in her mind, Bullard *was*, namely a person she deemed to be unworthy of further employment because of an expressed sympathy for black tenants. Dallman had, under our at-will employment law, the right to fire Bullard because she did not like people like him, people who are sympathetic to African-Americans. She had the right to fire him for any reason.[5]

And if he could be fired for any reason, so could Hammer, for associating with him. Two justices dissented on the ground that the discharge was for objecting to an illegal policy.

Neither the majority opinion nor the dissent considered whether the holding and (tepid) expression of social views inconsistent with the corporate management is an aspect of personal privacy and autonomy shielded from employer sanction and control.

## A. Labor Organization and Employee Protest

### *2. State Law*

In *Bravo v. Dolsen Cos.*,[6] the Supreme Court of Washington held that state's "Little Norris LaGuardia Act" to protect the rights of nonunionized agricultural workers to strike for union recognition. Threatening strikers with dismissal and videotaping them on their picket line were actionable in damages, and discharge for engagement in that activity was held to be a discharge violative of public policy.

Unlike agricultural workers, whom Congress placed outside the scheme of the National Labor Relations Act, managerial employees (like statutory supervisors) are included under the Act but denied the rights accorded to nonmanagerial (and nonsupervisory) employees on the theory that the Act recognized their undivided duty of loyalty owed to the

---

[3] *Id.* at 633.
[4] *Id.* at 632.
[5] *Id.* at 635.
[6] 888 P.2d 147 (Wash. 1995).

corporate hierarchy. Thus a manager, unlike a rank-and-file worker, could be discharged for engaging in organizational activity, such as the display of a pro-union button.

In *Drake v. Cheyenne Newspapers, Inc.*,[7] two editorial employees, whom the National Labor Relations Board had held to be managerial, refused to wear anti-union buttons as part of their employer's anti-union campaign and were discharged. They sought shelter under the free speech clause of the Wyoming Constitution, which is drafted as a guaranty of power to individuals rather than as a limit only on government. The Supreme Court of Wyoming acknowledged that prior precedent suggested that the state's guaranty of free speech would extend to private actors, but—citing to First Amendment cases decided by the U.S. Supreme Court—it opined that free speech does not extend to expression on private property. It held accordingly that "[t]erminating an at-will employee for exercising his right to free speech by refusing to follow a legal directive of an employer on the employer's premises during working hours does not violate public policy."[8]

The case would appear to be far more vexing than the court's brief treatment recognizes. The federal precedent cited concerned only the First Amendment's application to private actors. If the Wyoming Constitution is broader, a position that the court essays, then the federal precedent would be irrelevant. Moreover, the court's observation that the employer's order was lawful begs the question presented. More important, the court's refusal to extend the state's free speech clause to reach speech on the private employer's property and on work time necessarily implies that the free speech clause *would* extend to a private sector employee's speech off the employer's premises and on nonwork time. Insofar as the company would appear to have insisted on a duty of obedience by managerial employees as extensions of the corporate will, the jurisprudential basis for this distinction remains to be explained.

Suffice it to say that the company could insist that its managers not display a *pro*-union button, and refusal to abide by such an order, even if otherwise sheltered by Wyoming law, would seem to be preempted by federal law. But a refusal *to* display an anti-union message in public to which managers held conscientious objection would not seem to be spoken to by federal law. Had the managers refused on religious grounds there would seem to be little question that their employer would have reasonably had to accommodate their beliefs and, arguably, could not have insisted that they bear witness in public to a religiously repugnant message. There seems little obvious reason why the result would not be

---

[7]891 P.2d 80 (Wyo. 1995).

[8]*Id.* at 82.

the same under the state public policy, expressed in its constitution, if their objections were predicated on other grounds held with equal conscientiousness.

*a. Resort to Counsel.* The federal court for the Northern District of Iowa was presented with the question of whether an employee discharged for threatening to consult an attorney over her workplace dispute could state a claim for discharge in violation of public policy.[9] In a researched and well-reasoned opinion, the court concluded that she could:

> In light of the clear articulations of public policy favoring consultation with attorneys in order to determine whether a person has a legal problem, public policy favoring the availability of competent legal advice, public policy placing on lawyers a duty to counsel only actions that are legal and just, and public policy favoring compensation of legal counsel for individuals who endeavor to vindicate civil rights, the court concludes that acts that impede an individual from seeking legal advice would be "injurious to the public, or against the public good," would not be "right and just," and could potentially have a deleterious effect on "what affects the citizens of the State collectively." Such conduct would therefore be in violation of public policy. Even if the authorities cited above in support of the public policy did not exist, the court concludes that a consultation with a lawyer is so fundamental to our system of justice that an employer's discharge of an employee for consulting a lawyer would violate public policy. The court concludes that public policy protection extends to an at-will employee's statement of an intention to consult with an attorney concerning a dispute with an employer.[10]

The reasoning in *Thompto* was adopted by the Ohio Court of Appeals in considering the discharge of an employee who consulted an attorney who, in turn, wrote to demand that a reprimand be removed from the employee's file.[11] But the Appellate Court of Illinois held that an employee could be discharged because her son, a lawyer, was representing a party in a lawsuit against her employer[12] and the Oregon Court of Appeals held that an employee, suspected of theft, could be discharged for having called her lawyer.[13]

*b. Participating in a Lawsuit.* The prevailing view is that an employee may be discharged for participating in a lawsuit against his or her employer unless such participation is expressly sheltered by some

---

[9]Thompto v. Coborn's, Inc., 871 F. Supp. 1097, 10 IER Cases 263 (N.D. Iowa 1994).

[10]*Id.* at 1121.

[11]Simonelli v. Anderson Concrete Co., 650 N.E.2d 488, 11 IER Cases 236 (Ohio Ct. App. 1994).

[12]Paris v. Cherry Payment Sys., Inc., 638 N.E.2d 351, 9 IER Cases 1727 (Ill. App. Ct. 1994).

[13]Downs v. Waremart, 903 P.2d 888 (Or. App. 1995), *review allowed,* 909 P.2d 161 (Or. 1996).

protective or antiretaliation statute.[14] The Supreme Court of Oklahoma reviewed the extensive authority on point,[15] but concluded that an employee injured on the job by a customer of his employer could not be discharged for pursuing a statutory compensation claim against the customer any more than he could have been discharged for pursuing a claim against his employer directly. The dissenters argued that the employer had a right to protect its relationship to its customers, a relationship that could be threatened by the employee's lawsuit. To the majority, being compelled to give up a part of one's statutory claim to compensation

> in the face of an employer's threat of discharge is just as repugnant to the expressed *public policy* as is being forced into paying or contributing to the employer's compensation liability insurance premiums. In both instances it is the employee to whom the cost of on-the-job harm would be impermissibly shifted. That which the law prohibits the employer from exacting *contractually* may not be secured with impunity *through naked intimidation.*[16]

## B. Political Association and Expression

### *2. State Protection*

Absent some explicit treatment by statute or a close connection between the public purpose and private action, the courts tend to be highly sympathetic to the potentially adverse public relations aspects of employee political (and social) association and expression. In *Ribando v. Silhouette Optical, Ltd.,*[17] an executive of the company was discharged for having been elected mayor of a locality in New York. The court held no cause of action available under the state's human rights law, the only ground arguable in New York (inasmuch as the state has not recognized a general tort for a discharge in violation of public policy):

> Caution is indicated where courts are asked to interpolate such a category as a right to continuation of private employment at an executive level even if the employer objects to the employee's acceptance of an executive level public office. While blanket moonlighting prohibitions, especially if not uniformly and evenhandedly enforced, may at times be suspect . . . an executive level public servant is almost certain to attract both favorable and unfavorable attention. Unfavorable reactions to the person of a marketing executive may well risk causing adverse business consequences to the executive's employer.

---

[14]*See* King v. Driscoll, 638 N.E.2d 488, 9 IER Cases 1475 (Mass. 1994) (shareholder derivative suit); Shearson Lehman Bros. v. Hedrich, 639 N.E.2d 228, 9 IER Cases 1826 (Ill. App. Ct. 1994) (dictum); *cf.* Minnesota Ass'n of Nurse Anesthetists v. Unity Hosp., 59 F.3d 80 (8th Cir. 1995) (dictum to the effect that coworker participation in a whistleblower lawsuit not statutorily protected).

[15]Groce v. Foster, 880 P.2d 902, 907–08 n.34, 9 IER Cases 1287 (Okla. 1994).

[16]880 P.2d at 906 (footnote omitted).

[17]871 F. Supp. 675 (S.D.N.Y. 1994).

> Controversy inherent in executive office in the public sector may also divert the core of the incumbent's attention away from private sector duties. These are adequate reasons for an employer to object to coexistence of potentially incompatible executive positions such as were sought by plaintiff.[18]

The potential conflict became palpable when Lawrence Korb, a former assistant secretary of defense in the Reagan administration and a lobbyist for a defense contractor, was dismissed for having given a speech urging a scaling back of Navy plans for a 600-ship, 15-carrier-group Navy.[19] He sought relief under Article 16 of the Massachusetts Declaration of Rights assuring that "[t]he right of free speech shall not be abridged." The Supreme Court of Massachusetts disagreed that such relief was available, albeit only on the precise facts of the case:

> Korb characterizes the public policy at issue too broadly. His situation is not that of an employee who is fired for speaking out on issues in which his employer has no interest, financial or otherwise. To the contrary, Korb was hired to be the corporation's spokesperson, and he spoke against the interest of the corporation. The topic was one of acute concern to Raytheon. Regardless of whether Korb believed himself to be acting privately rather than as a Raytheon employee, and regardless of what Korb actually said, the public perception after the press conference was that a Raytheon lobbyist advocated a reduction in defense spending. Raytheon had a financial stake in not advocating that position.

"Therefore, it determined that Korb had lost his effectiveness as its spokesperson. There is no public policy prohibiting an employer from discharging an ineffective at-will employee. The fact that Korb's job duties included public speaking does not alter this rule."[20]

The question was presented in Pennsylvania on a narrower issue and in the context of a covenant not to compete.[21] The defendant had been employed (apparently as an accountant) under a contract of employment that contained a covenant not to compete (with a damage clause) if the employee was dismissed for cause and entered into competition. Cause was defined as including, but not limited to "moral turpitude, being charged with a felony, use of illicit drugs, intoxication while working, insulting Employer's family and clients, not working, intentionally working slowly, intentionally losing clients, engaging in sexual activities in the office, and homosexuality."[22] The employee appeared on a local television station to defend gays and lesbians, was discharged, entered into competition in violation of the covenant, and was sued successfully

[18] *Id.* at 677 (citation omitted).
[19] Korb v. Raytheon Corp., 574 N.E.2d 370, 6 IER Cases 1002 (Mass. 1991).
[20] *Id.* at 372 (footnote omitted).
[21] DeMuth v. Miller, 652 A. 2d 891 (Pa. Super. Ct. 1995).
[22] *Id.* at 892–93.

under the damage clause. To the appellate court, the issue was not the defendant's homosexuality but his breach of the noncompetition clause. It cited the employer's testimony at trial that

> the defendant was not discharged only because of his sexual predilections. It was the fact that the defendant communicated on a local television station his views concerning a controversial issue (gay and lesbian bashing on behalf of a Harrisburg organization opposed to such conduct). The plaintiff believed that such outspoken remarks by the defendant would be imputed to the business because of the defendant's employee status. Further, clients and prospective clients might be offended by the remarks and choose not to do business with the plaintiff's firm.[23]

Over dissent, the court declined to hold that the enforcement of the contractual provision implicated any consideration of equal protection under the Fourteenth Amendment.

### C. Religious Association and Expression

In *Wilson v. U.S. West Communications,*[24] an employee of long standing, a devout Roman Catholic, took a religious vow that she would wear an anti-abortion button until there was an end to abortion or until she could no longer fight. The button, two inches in diameter, depicted a color photograph of a fetus, 18 to 20 weeks old. It caused considerable disruption among her coworkers—some for personal reasons having nothing to do with abortion, such as miscarriage, premature infant death, or infertility—who threatened to walk off the job. The employer offered three options: (1) wear the button only in her work cubicle, (2) cover it while at work, or (3) omit the photograph—the major source of coworker objection. She declined these as inconsistent with her vow and argued that the company ought to focus on her coworkers, not on her (i.e., just tell them to do their work). The Eighth Circuit held that the wearing of the button was the result of genuinely held religious belief, but that the accommodation offered by the employer was reasonable. The court rejected her claim that her vow required the public display of the message in contradistinction to the wearing of it; thus, the court opined, wearing it covered would accommodate her religious vow and assuage her coworkers.

The reverse situation was presented in *Meltebeke v. Bureau of Labor and Industries,*[25] of an employer's claim of a right to subject employees to religious "witnessing" under the Constitution of the State of Oregon. The state antidiscrimination agency had adopted rules governing religious

---

[23] *Id.* at 899.

[24] 58 F.3d 1337 (8th Cir. 1995).

[25] 903 P.2d 351 (Or. App. 1995), *review allowed,* 909 P.2d 161 (Or. 1996).

harassment on the job, modeled on the EEOC's rules on sexual harassment,[26] and applied them to a sole proprietor of a painting business, an evangelical Christian who held it a religious duty to tell his employee that the employee was a sinner who was damned to hell because he was sleeping with his fiancee and because he didn't attend church. The Supreme Court of Oregon sustained the rule under Oregon's robust free expression of religion clause, but held it required a showing of actual knowledge by the employer that its practice had the harassing effect forbidden by the rule.

## D. Other Sodalities

### *1. Community Service*

The Pennsylvania Emergency Medical Services Act provides in pertinent part:

> No first responder, emergency medical technician or EMT-paramedic who in good faith attempts to render emergency care authorized by this act at an emergency scene while en route to a place of employment shall receive any form of reprimand or penalty by an employer as a result of late arrival at the place of employment. An employer may request written verification from any such first responder, emergency medical technician or EMT-paramedic, who shall obtain the written verification from either the police officer or ambulance personnel who is in charge at the emergency scene.[27]

When an employee, a Certified Emergency Medical Technician (EMT), was late for work because of having stopped at an accident scene on his way to work to render emergency aid, he was, he alleged, reprimanded by his employer, demoted to an entry-level position, and told that he would have to choose between his job as an EMT and his employment with his employer.[28] (The court does not indicate whether or not his tardiness was a recurrent event because of his EMT service.) He sued for infliction of emotional distress. His action against his employer was held preempted by the exclusivity provision of the state's

---

[26]The rule provided in pertinent part that:

> An employer commits an unfair labor practice if the employer, because of an employee's religion, makes religious advances and other physical or verbal conduct that are
> (1) in fact unwelcome by the employee; and
> (2) have the purpose or effect of
> (a) unreasonably interfering with the subject's work performance; or
> (b) creating a working environment that a reasonable person would find intimidating, hostile, or offensive.

[27]PA. STAT. ch. 35, §6931(j)(5).

[28]Snyder v. Specialty Glass Prods., Inc., 658 A.2d 366 (Pa. Super. Ct. 1995).

workers' compensation law, and the action against the individual defendants was held not to have presented an actionable claim. He had not alleged a violation of the Act, but the court said that such could not have been presented inasmuch as he had not suffered any "economic loss."[29] However, the court's dictum on the scope of Section 6931(j)(5) seems to ignore the Act's reference to "*any* form of reprimand or penalty" (emphasis added).

Where the community service at issue involves association with persons who are disabled within the meaning of the Americans With Disabilities Act, it is arguable that such activity is statutorily protected under that Act which defines impermissible "discrimination" by a statutory "covered entity" to reach "excluding or otherwise denying equal jobs or benefits to a qualified individual because of the known disability of an individual with whom the qualified individual is known to have a relationship or association."[30] Thus it is arguable that discharge for assisting in an AIDS clinic would violate the Act.

## II. INDIVIDUAL AUTONOMY

### A. Intimate and Personal Relationships

In *Green v. Bryant*,[31] the employee alleged that she was discharged by her employer from a medical practice when the employer learned that she had been raped and beaten by her husband, from whom she had been separated. (The court speculated that the employer's reason stemmed from concern for the emotional or even physical well-being of other employees and patients if the husband engaged in other violent activity toward the plaintiff at the workplace.) Her actions for emotional distress and discharge violative of public policy were dismissed for failure to state a claim. Of the latter, relying on Pennsylvania criminal law governing protection against abuse and providing for the compensation of crime victims, the court opined:

> It might be a different case, and a closer question as to the public policy exception, if plaintiff alleged that she was discharged because she had applied for victim compensation or had sought a protective order. That, however, is not her allegation. . . . Therefore, in the absence of any indication that Pennsylvania has established a clear mandate that crime victims generally, or spousal abuse victims specifically, are entitled to benefits or privileges beyond those

---

[29] *Id.* at 372.

[30] 42 U.S.C. §12112(b)(4) (1995 Supp.).

[31] 887 F. Supp. 798, 10 IER Cases 1179 (E.D. Pa. 1995).

enumerated in the laws, I must conclude that plaintiff's dismissal was not in violation of public policy.[32]

### *1. Marriage*

Marital status is not considered as invidious ground absent connection to some other statutory scheme, notably an express provision in state antidiscrimination law. Thus, a father's firing his son because of the son's marriage outside the faith was held to work no invasion of privacy;[33] the discharge of a bank officer because of the fear of adverse publicity and loss of customer confidence resulting from the arrest of her husband for misappropriating funds at another bank was held to state no claim for sex discrimination;[34] the discharge of an insurance representative because her husband took a job with a competitor stated no cause of action;[35] and the discharge of a mother because her son, a lawyer, was counsel in a lawsuit against the employer stated no cause of action.[36]

In *Magula v. Benton Franklin Title Insurance Co.*,[37] a female employee was discharged because her husband, a contractor for her employer, had been making threatening telephone calls to her coworker because of the coworker's charge of misconduct leveled against the husband. The Washington Court of Appeals held the claim to state a cause of action under the inclusion of marital status as a protected category in employment discrimination, even though the discharge would not have been actionable had it been due to disruption resulting from the same allegations of misconduct made about a relative other than a spouse.

A refusal to hire predicated on the race of a spouse has been held actionable under federal civil rights law, but the Oklahoma Court of Appeals refused to extend the state's tort law to reach those facts (in a case where the statute of limitations on the civil rights action had expired).[38]

*a. Antinepotism Policies.* Metro Health Medical Center, an Ohio county hospital, had a finely tuned antinepotism policy:

IX. *NEPOTISM*

A. In order to prevent conflicts which may arise in situations where members of the same immediate family are employed by the Hospital, the Hospital will

---

[32]*Id.* at 801. It should be noted California allows an employer to seek an injunction against a potentially hostile person coming on the premises in its Workplace Violence Safety Act, CAL. CIV. PROC. CODE §527.8 (1996 Supp.).

[33]Frankel v. Warwick Hotel, 881 F. Supp. 183, 10 IER Cases 918 (E.D. Pa. 1995).

[34]Panis v. Mission Hills Bank, 60 F.3d 1486 (10th Cir. 1995).

[35]Berry v. Liberty Nat'l Life Ins. Co., 879 F. Supp. 44 (S.D. Miss. 1995).

[36]Paris v. Cherry Payment Sys., Inc., 638 N.E.2d 351, 9 IER Cases 1727 (Ill. App. Ct. 1994).

[37]901 P.2d 313 (Wash. Ct. App. 1995), *review granted*, 910 P.2d 482 (Wash. 1996).

[38]Williams v. Dub Ross Co., 895 P.2d 1344, 10 IER Cases 1268 (Okla. Ct. App. 1995).

not allow an individual to be employed, transferred or promoted, where as a result, any of the following situations would exist:

> 3. Members of the same immediate family being in positions which are of such close proximity that they would necessarily interact with each other in the performance of their duties.

C. If, as a result of a marriage between two employees, a violation of the Nepotism guidelines arises, the affected employees will be given the option of electing which spouse will be moved to another position in the Hospital System so as to eliminate the nepotism violation. If no election is made by either spouse in thirty (30) calendar days after notice to the employees, the least senior in terms of Hospital seniority will be moved. All reasonable attempts will be made to insure that the displaced employee is given a position of comparable responsibility and pay.[39]

When a nurse assigned to the hospital's emergency airlift medical service run by a contractor, Life Flight, married the Life Flight helicopter pilot with whom she worked, the employer called the policy into effect and the couple challenged it on constitutional and state law grounds. The U.S. Court of Appeals for the Sixth Circuit found no infirmity in the policy.

The Eleventh Circuit considered a more broadly framed rule governing the police department of Warner Robins, Georgia.[40] The policy prohibited any person from working in any city department where a relative of that person occupied a supervisory position. The rule was sustained against constitutional attack (and upon a full review of authority elsewhere) on the ground of the city's justification for it, that is "avoiding conflicts of interest between work-related and family-related obligations; reducing favoritism or even the appearance of favoritism; preventing family conflicts from affecting the workplace; and, by limiting interoffice dating, decreasing the likelihood of sexual harassment in the workplace."[41]

*b. Extramarital Relationships.* Two cases presented the question of the employer's liability to wronged spouses for extramarital affairs conducted by the employee/spouse. The first, *Helena Laboratories Corp. v. Snyder,*[42] arose in the context of the legislature's abolition of a cause of action for alienation of affection. The intermediate appellate court had cast the case in terms of a failure of corporate supervision, to which the legislature's action did not speak:

> [T]he workplace should be just that, a place where employees perform the usual duties of their jobs. Spouses should be secure in the knowledge that employers will not condone the type activity involved in this case between its

---

[39]Wright v. Metrohealth Medical Ctr., 58 F.3d 1130, 1132–33, 10 IER Cases 1418 (6th Cir. 1995).

[40]Parks v. City of Warner Robins, Ga., 43 F.3d 609, 11 IER Cases 397 (11th Cir. 1995).

[41]43 F.3d at 615.

[42]886 S.W.2d 767, 10 IER Cases 10 (Tex. 1994).

> employees. Spouses should be secure in the knowledge that when employers discover those type of activities are happening on their premises or during working hours, those employers will take reasonable steps, within their means, to prevent a tortious invasion of the family interest. Spouses should be secure in the knowledge that when employers breach this duty, courts will provide a remedy.[43]

The dissenting intermediate appellate judge thought the majority was inviting the employer's intervention into the personal affairs of its employees. The Texas Supreme Court avoided resolving this conflict by holding the action precluded by the abolition of the tort of alienation of affection; that is, allowing the action to proceed would subject the employer to liability for the employee's conduct for which the employee could not be held liable.

Utah, however, retains the tort of alienation of affection, and the Supreme Court of Utah confronted the same type of claim presented by the husband of an employee who had had an affair with two corporate executives (i.e., of both that tort and a failure to supervise).[44] The court read the requirements of the tort narrowly in the employment setting:

> The tort will not lie when the personalities or inadequacies of the spouses, not the acts of third persons, caused the breakdown of the bonds that are essential to the consortium interests protected by law. . . . Romantic relationships between employees may only be incidental to, or result from, the primary causes of marital discord and loss of affections. . . . Thus, an employer's awareness of a romantic relationship between two of its employees does not give the employer sufficient knowledge to anticipate a claim for alienation of affections against an employee under its supervision.[45]

The court addressed the negligence claim in terms virtually identical to those of the dissent in the intermediate appellate court in Texas:

> Policy considerations also preclude our imposition of a duty upon employers to police the private conduct of their employees for the protection of employees' spouses. The cause of action for alienation of affections provides a remedy when a third person is at fault for the destruction of a marital relation. . . . We decline to extend its reach to impose a duty upon employers to control their employees' private relationships.
>
> In addition, employers have no duty to determine the marital status of their employees. It would be unreasonable to impose upon employers a duty to monitor romantic relationships among their employees to protect marital relations of which they may not even be aware. Indeed, absent some indication of harassment or intimidation, an employer who attempted, merely upon the basis of its knowledge of a romantic relationship, to police the personal conduct

[43]Snyder v. Helena Lab., Inc., 877 S.W.2d 35, 37 n.2 (Tex. Ct. App. 1994).
[44]Jackson v. Righter, 891 P.2d 1387 (Utah 1995).
[45]*Id.* at 1393.

of its employees may expose itself to liability for interfering with private relationships.[46]

The permissibility of a public employer's denial of a promotion to a police officer for having an affair with a fellow officer's wife was considered in *City of Sherman v. Henry*,[47] under the state constitution's right of privacy. The court held the action unconstitutional—for want of a carefully tailored regulation or rule promulgated in advance and for want of an adequate demonstration of a compelling interest to support the prohibition.

### *3. Nonfraternization*

An employee's claim of wrongful discharge for having maintained a "social relationship" with a coworker whom she later married was held to state a claim for marital discrimination cognizable under the Illinois human rights act (which includes "marital status" as a proscribed ground).[48] The court did not discuss whether or not an employer could sanction such a social relationship absent marriage.[49]

### *4. Sexual Relationships Outside the Company*

In *State v. Wal-Mart Stores, Inc.*,[50] the court considered the application of New York's statutory prohibition against discharge or discrimination due to engagement in "legal recreational activities outside work hours" and held it inapplicable to a prohibition on coworker dating.[51]

The statute was considered by a federal district court in *Pasch v. Katz Media Corp.*,[52] concerning its application to a demotion for cohabiting with a former executive employee of the employer. The court extensively reviewed the legislative history of the measure, including the vetoes of previous legislative efforts, and concluded:

> [The] legislative history shows that the purpose of the statute is to prohibit employers from discriminating against their employees simply because the employer does not like the activities an employee engages in after work. The legislative history indicates the statute was intended to include social activities,

---

[46] *Id.* at 1393–94.

[47] 910 S.W.2d 542 (Tex. Ct. App. 1995).

[48] Talley v. Washington Inventory Serv., 37 F.3d 310, 9 IER Cases 1729 (7th Cir. 1994).

[49] In Clark v. Chick-Fil-A, Inc., 449 S.E.2d 313 (Ga. Ct. App. 1994), a franchisee's resignation was demanded because he had cohabited with a supervisory employee. The company took this conduct to hold the company to "public scandal and ridicule" forbidden by the franchise contract. *Id.* at 314. The plaintiff resigned, and this resignation could not be challenged under Georgia law on any ground of undue pressure.

[50] 621 N.Y.S.2d 158, 10 IER Cases 255 (App. Div. 1995).

[51] The statute is discussed in Chapter 6 of the main volume at §II.C.1.

[52] 10 IER Cases 1574 (S.D.N.Y. 1995).

whether or not they have a romantic element, so long as the activity occurs outside work hours, off of the employer's premises and without use of the employer's equipment or other property; and does not create a material conflict of interest related to the employer's trade secrets, proprietary information, or other proprietary or business interest. The Court therefore reaches a conclusion similar to that of Justice Yesawich, the dissenting judge in *Wal-Mart*. . . .[53]

### *5. Homosexuality*

The California Court of Appeals has held that discharge because of the employee's homosexuality states a claim under California law as a violation of public policy stated in state antidiscrimination law, which action need not hinge upon the exhaustion of administrative remedies under that law.[54] However, the court rejected the claim that such action worked an invasion of privacy. California's constitutional guaranty of privacy has been read by the California Supreme Court to recognize two classes of interests: "(1) interests in precluding the dissemination or misuse of sensitive and confidential information ('informational privacy'); and (2) interests in making intimate personal decisions or conducting personal activities without observation, intrusion, or interference ('autonomy privacy').[55]

The first category was not implicated, the court opined, because the plaintiff's homosexuality was not confidential; it was rather well known, whence his allegations of harassment. Neither was the second: "In discussing the autonomy privacy interest, our Supreme Court has specifically recognized that the state constitutional right of privacy was not intended 'to create any unbridled right of personal freedom of action that may be vindicated in lawsuits against either government agencies or private persons or entities.' "[56]

### *6. Friendships and Interpersonal Association*

In *Glasgow v. Sherwin-Williams Co.*,[57] a long-standing store manager was dismissed, and the employer directed its employees not to associate with him. He contested that order as a violation of his right to privacy.

---

[53] *Id.* at 1578. Justice Yesawich had opined that

> given the fact that the legislature's primary intent . . . was to curtail employers' ability to discrimination on the basis of activities . . . that have no bearing on one's ability to perform one's job, and concomitantly to guarantee employees a certain degree of freedom to conduct their lives as they please during nonworking hours, the narrow interpretation adopted by the majority is indefensible.

State v. Wal-Mart Stores, 621 N.Y.S.2d 158, 160 (Yesawich, J., dissenting).

[54] Liebert v. Transworld Sys., Inc., 39 Cal. Rptr. 2d 65 (Cal. Ct. App. 1995).

[55] *Id.* at 69.

[56] *Id.*

[57] 901 F. Supp. 1185 (N.D. Miss. 1995).

The court disagreed: No reasonable jury, it held, would find the order objectionable in the sense of being of so "highly offensive [a] nature" as the tort of intrusion into one's seclusion requires.[58] As a result, no inquiry was made as to the employer's reason for the directive.

Slightly more attention to that question was given in *Thelen v. Marc's Big Boy Corp.*,[59] in which the plaintiff alleged that he had been discharged in a managerial purge of contemporaries of the company's former president. The Seventh Circuit held that discharge for such association was inactionable:

> There is no "well-defined public policy" against a new company president removing those he perceives to be less than faithful to him. Such practices are not uncommon in the business world. The business judgment rule gives managers wide latitude to decide what is in the best interest of a company—without the judiciary peeking over their collective shoulders.[60]

## B. Grooming and Dress

In *Lee v. Levi Strauss & Co.*,[61] two former employees of a supplier of Levi Strauss sued the company for tortious interference in contract, in conditioning its future purchases from their employer upon their discharge. Several of Levi Strauss's plant managers had complained of their failure to call on the plant, their failure properly to sign entry logs when they did call, and the habit of one of them of wearing sunglasses during business dealings. The court held the grounds asserted by Strauss to provide legal justification:

> Levi Strauss had the right to insist that Threads [the supplier/employer] employees comply with its security procedures (i.e. signing in when sales representatives made calls on Levi Strauss plants), the right to service by Threads representatives on its contracts, the right to work with Threads representatives *who demeaned themselves in a manner Levi Strauss deemed appropriate*, the right to work with Threads representatives who were responsive to its needs, and the right to insist that Threads provide representatives who met these criteria.
>
> Furthermore, we conclude that Levi Strauss could insist that Appellants not be involved in the servicing of its contracts. Inasmuch as the record reflects that these two gentlemen were the only personnel in the El Paso office, it is only rational that in the exercise of its contractual rights, Levi could insist that Appellants be fired. . . . To hold otherwise would entail absurd results. Economic relationships between companies are vital components in our society. Employees of companies with ongoing business relations should be subject to discharge upon complaints by a customer company, and they should expect such requests if their personal performance is substandard. Employees are

---

[58] *Id.* at 1192–93.
[59] 64 F.3d 264 (7th Cir. 1995).
[60] *Id.* at 270.
[61] 897 S.W.2d 501 (Tex. Ct. App. 1995).

protected from improper discharge in this setting by discrimination in employment statutes, the terms of their employment contracts, and the "*bona fide* exercise" qualification on the affirmative defense of legal justification.[62]

A demand by a customer not to be served by a member of a class protected by federal or state law could not be acceded to by an employer, and if an employee's wearing of sunglasses could not provide a basis for employer discipline directly, neither could the employer accomplish that end by acceding to the customer's demand. But only the District of Columbia thus far makes personal appearance a protected category.

*1. Constitutional Protection in Public Employment*

In *Francis v. Keane,*[63] uniformed correctional officers who were Rastafarians challenged their employer's order to cut their (modified) dreadlocks on grounds of the First Amendment, the Religious Freedom Restoration Act,[64] and state constitutional law. The federal district court held the employer's general allegations of safety, discipline, and *esprit de corps* insufficient to grant the employer summary judgment.

*2. Antidiscrimination Law*

*c. Religious discrimination.* In *Kohli v. LOOC, Inc.,*[65] the Maryland Court of Special Appeals considered the failure of Domino's Pizza to hire a Sikh as a store manager due to his refusal, based on the tenets of Sikhism, to shave his beard. The case had been heard by an administrative law judge of the Maryland Commission on Human Relations, who found for the applicant. Her decision was reversed by the Commission's Appeal Board whose decision was affirmed by the lower court. The Court of Special Appeals held that both the Appeals Board and the lower court had failed to follow the proper standard of review of an ALJ's decision under Maryland law, and remanded the case to the agency.

*3. Common Law*

In *Advanced Mobilehome Systems v. Unemployment Appeals Comm'n,*[66] the Florida Court of Appeals reversed the determination of the Commission and denied unemployment compensation to an employee who quit rather than shave a three-day growth of beard as required by his employer's grooming policy. The employee was a roofer; his employer

---

[62] *Id.* at 505 (emphasis added).
[63] 888 F. Supp. 568 (S.D.N.Y. 1995).
[64] 42 U.S.C. §200066 et seq.
[65] 654 A.2d 922 (Md. 1995).
[66] 663 So. 2d 1382 (Fla. Dist. Ct. App. 1995).

worked primarily on the installation of roofs on mobile homes. The court stressed that the constitutional protection for individual liberty in matters of dress and grooming did not extend to private employers. The court found the reasons given for the grooming policy to be justified by a

> legitimate business interest in ensuring its reputation among its customers. Specifically, claimant's duties involved contact with customers when he went to their homes. He would introduce himself, answer their questions and collect the bill when work was completed. The employees work outside and are visible to anyone who happens to pass by.[67]

*a. Undress.* In *Schonauer v. DCR Entertainment,*[68] the court held that persistent pressure by the management of a topless nightclub to persuade a waitress to participate in a "nude waitress contest" constituted actionable sexual harassment under the state's antidiscrimination law.

## C. Other Off-Duty Conduct

### *1. Recreation*

In *Tindle v. Caudell,*[69] an off-duty Little Rock police officer attended a Halloween party at the Fraternal Order of Police dressed in blackface and carrying a watermelon. Although he intended his costume as a joke, it was not taken that way by some black members of the department and by the department itself. Tindle was suspended for 30 days, which action was sustained as against challenge under the First Amendment. The Eighth Circuit agreed that forms of dress can perform a communicative function but stated that

> Tindle does not suggest that he wore his costume to express a message. He has not, for example, asserted a claim that he wore it to incite debate, to alienate others, to comment on an issue, or even to send a racist message. In fact, he testified to the Civil Service Commission that he wore it strictly to "have a good time." He specifically denied having the intent to belittle, taunt, mock, degrade or offend anyone.[70]

Nor could his dress be considered as a form of entertainment worthy of First Amendment protection—he did not perform in a skit or in any sort of theatrical performance,[71] and his appearance was not part of a costume contest. He intended, in other words, to express no message, and the

---

[67] *Id.* at 1388.

[68] 905 P.2d 392 (Wash. Ct. App. 1995).

[69] 56 F.3d 966, 10 IER Cases 1227 (8th Cir. 1995).

[70] 56 F.3d at 969.

[71] *Distinguishing* Berger v. Battaglia, 779 F.2d 992 (4th Cir. 1985), *cert. denied*, 476 U.S. 1159 (1986).

absence of this intention attenuates any claim of First Amendment protection. Consequently, the court held his behavior to lack any statement on an issue of public concern necessary to implicate the Free Speech Clause.

Alternatively, and relying heavily on the special function and form of organization of police departments, the court opined that the department's need for harmony and close working relationships trumped Tindle's right to dress as he chose at the party:

> [I]t is undisputed that some African-American officers of the LRPD [Little Rock Police Department] were offended by Tindle's costume. That race relations were a concern of the LRPD is evidenced by the fact that it had retained an expert to conduct prejudice reduction workshops. Moreover, Tindle did not intend to convey a message by his costume. He wore it in a private setting, limiting any possible public interest in his expression. Although Tindle was off-duty during the party, his appearance was witnessed by police officers and their guests. There was the potential for more direct consequences to the department than if he had attended a family or neighborhood party in the costume. Under all the circumstances Tindle's interest in appearing as he chose at the party does not outweigh the countervailing interests in maintaining discipline and harmonious working relationships within the LRPD.[72]

## D. Other Aspects of Individual Personality

### *2. Abrasiveness*

Given the very high legal standard for liability for infliction of emotional distress, an employer is not liable for the abrasive, obnoxious, and childish remarks and behavior of supervisors and coworkers unless they create impermissibly hostile environments actionable under employment discrimination laws or rise to a level of utter intolerability.[73] Where, for example, a manager motivated his sales force by the use of intimidating and abusive language—using such phrases with his subordinates as "miserable sack of shit," "I'll rip out your fucking heart," "ruin you emotionally and financially," "ruin your family," make you "suck dick"—a management tactic he called "mind fucking," the court held it to be a jury question whether this conduct exceeded all bounds of social tolerability.[74] Neither, however, is such an employee protected from discharge on the ground

---

[72]56 F.3d at 972, relying on Pruitt v. Howard County Sheriff's Dep't, 623 A.2d 696 (Md. Ct. Spec. App.), *cert. denied*, 630 A.2d 723 (Md. 1993), *cert. denied*, 114 S. Ct. 1059 (1994).

[73]*See, e.g.*, Coville v. Cobarc Servs., Inc., 869 P.2d 1103 (Wash. Ct. App. 1994) (encountering a supervisor masturbating in a remote room is not sexual harassment); Lawson v. Heidelberg E., 872 F. Supp. 335 (N.D. Miss.), *aff'd*, 70 F.3d 1269 (5th Cir. 1995); Bolden v. PRC, Inc., 43 F.3d 545 (10th Cir. 1994); Howry v. Nisus, Inc., 910 F. Supp. 576 (M.D. Fla. 1995).

[74]Blackthorne v. Posner, 883 F. Supp. 1443 (D. Or. 1995).

of such behavior,[75] which may at a certain point justify the denial of unemployment benefits. As it was put in one such case:

> In the three months plaintiff was employed by ADM he alienated five different auditors to the point where they did not want to work with him. He accomplished this by cursing at them, shoving them against a wall and throwing files at them. Plaintiff acknowledged he had been told after the initial incident of shoving and cursing he must learn to get along with co-workers or he would be terminated. Wilful behavior stems from employee awareness of a company rule that is disregarded by the employee. . . . Common sense implies the existence of a policy against not only physical threats and violence but also throwing objects at supervisors even if plaintiff had not been warned about getting along with fellow workers.[76]

### *3. Indecency*

A university women's gymnastics coach who videotaped himself and his wife having sexual intercourse, using a portion of a videotape that was also used to record gymnastic events and that he knew his students would review, was properly dismissed for cause.[77] Even if the subsequent display of the tape was unintentional, the court opined that his conduct was inconsistent with his role in the university.

Where an employee entered a special supervision program resulting from an act of public indecency (in exposing himself to a child), his discharge—the ground of which was authorized in a "Letter of Understanding Relating to Sex Crimes" negotiated with his union—could not be contested as wrongful under state law.[78]

---

[75] *See, e.g.*, Kahn v. United States Secretary of Labor, 64 F.3d 271 (7th Cir. 1995).

[76] Lachenmyer v. Didrickson, 636 N.E.2d 93, 99 (Ill. App. Ct. 1994).

[77] Deli v. University of Minn., 511 N.W.2d 46 (Minn. Ct. App. 1994).

[78] Klein v. Boeing Co., 847 F. Supp. 838 (W.D. Wash. 1994).

# Part II

## Statutory and Regulatory References

# POLYGRAPHY AND LIE DETECTION

## II. State Legislation

### O. Montana (as amended in 1995)

*Mont. Code Ann. §39-2-304 (1995)*

**Sec. 39-2-304. Lie detector tests prohibited—regulation of blood and urine testing.** (1) A person, firm, corporation, or other business entity or its representative may not require:

(a) as a condition for employment or continuation of employment, a person to take a polygraph test or any form of a mechanical lie detector test;

(b) as a condition for employment, a person to submit to a blood or urine test, except for employment in:

(i) hazardous work environments;

(ii) jobs the primary responsibility of which is security, public safety, or fiduciary responsibility; or

(iii) jobs involving the intrastate commercial transportation of persons or commodities by a commercial motor carrier or an employee subject to driver qualification requirements; and

(c) as a condition for continuation of employment, an employee to submit to a blood or urine test, except when:

(i) the employer has reason to believe that the employee's faculties are impaired on the job as a result of alcohol consumption or illegal drug use;

(ii) the employer has reason to believe that an employee may have contributed to a work-related accident that causes death or personal injury or property damage in excess of $1,500; or

(iii) drug testing is being conducted at an employee's regular biennial physical for employment in jobs involving the intrastate commercial motor carrier transportation of persons or commodities.

(2) Prior to the administration of a drug or alcohol test, the person, firm, corporation, or other business entity or its representative shall adopt the written testing procedure that is provided in 49 CFR, part 40, and make it available to all persons subject to testing.

(3) The person, firm, corporation, or other business entity or its representative shall provide a copy of drug or alcohol test results to the person tested and provide the person with the opportunity, at the expense of the person

requiring the test, to obtain a confirmatory test of the blood or urine by an independent laboratory selected by the person tested. The person tested must be given the opportunity to rebut or explain the results of either test or both tests. In the case of an accident referred to in subsection (1)(c)(ii), the tests may not be delayed, but the person, firm, corporation, or other business entity or its representative shall, as soon as possible, make a written finding as to whether the act or failure to act is believed to be a direct or proximate cause of the accident and shall provide the tested employee with a copy of the finding. The written record of a blood or urine test of an employee who is required to submit to testing pursuant to subsection (1)(c)(ii) and whose acts or failure to act is subsequently found not to be the direct or proximate cause of a work-related accident must be removed from the employee's work record and be destroyed.

(4) Adverse action may not be taken against a person tested under subsections (1)(b), (1)(c), (2), and (3) if the person tested presents a reasonable explanation or medical opinion indicating that the results of the test were not caused by alcohol consumption or illegal drug use.

(5) A person who violates this section is guilty of a misdemeanor.

(6) As used in this section:

(a) "commercial motor carrier" has the meaning provided in 61-1-320 and in 69-12-101; and

(b) "intrastate" means commerce or trade that is begun, carried on, and completed wholly in this state.

# DRUG TESTING

## I. State Legislation

### O. Alabama

*Alabama Code §§25-5-330–340 (1995 Cum. Supp.)*

**Sec. 25-5-330. Legislative intent.** It is the intent of the Legislature to promote drug-free workplaces in order that employers in this state be afforded the opportunity to maximize their levels of productivity, enhance their competitive positions in the marketplace, and reach their desired levels of success without experiencing the costs, delays, and tragedies associated with work related accidents resulting from substance abuse by employees.

**Sec. 25-5-331. Definitions.** As used in this article, the following words and terms shall have meanings as follows:

(1) Alcohol. Ethyl alcohol, hydrated oxide of ethyl, or spirits of wine, from whatever source or by whatever process produced.

(2) Chain of custody. The methodology of tracking specified materials, specimens, or substances for the purpose of maintaining control and accountability from initial collection to final disposition for all of the materials, specimens, or substances and providing for accountability at each stage in handling, testing, and storing materials, specimens, or substances and reporting test results.

(3) Confirmation test or Confirmed test. A second analytical procedure used to identify the presence of a specific drug or metabolite in a specimen. The confirmation test shall be different in scientific principle from that of the initial test procedure. The confirmation method shall be capable of providing requisite specificity, sensitivity, and quantitative accuracy.

(4) Drug. Amphetamines, cannabinoids, cocaine, phencyclidine (PCP), methadone, methaqualone, opiates, barbituates, benzodiazepines, propoxyphene, or a metabolite of any of the substances.

(5) Employee. Any person who works for salary, wages, or other remuneration for an employer.

(6) Employee assistance program. A program designed to assist in the identification and resolution of job performance problems associated with employees impaired by personal concerns. A minimum level of core services shall include consultation and training; professional, confidential, appropriate, and timely problem assessment services; short-term problem

resolution; referrals for appropriate diagnosis, treatment, and assistance; follow-up and monitoring; employee education; and quality assurance.

(7) EMPLOYER. A person or entity that is subject to the Alabama Workers' Compensation Law, except that this article shall not apply to individual self-insurers or members of group self-insurance funds.

(8) INITIAL TEST. A sensitive, rapid, and reliable procedure to identify negative and presumptive positive specimens. All initial tests shall use an immunoassay procedure or an equivalent procedure or shall use a more accurate scientifically accepted method approved by the National Institute on Drug Abuse as more accurate technology becomes available in a cost-effective form.

(9) JOB APPLICANT. A person who has applied for a position with an employer and has been offered employment conditioned upon successfully passing a substance abuse test and may have begun work pending the results of the substance abuse test.

(10) NONPRESCRIPTION MEDICATION. A drug or medication authorized pursuant to federal or state law for general distribution and use without a prescription in the treatment of human disease, ailments, or injuries.

(11) PRESCRIPTION MEDICATION. A drug or medication lawfully prescribed by a physician for an individual and taken in accordance with the prescription.

(12) REASONABLE SUSPICION TESTING. Substance abuse testing based on a belief that an employee is using or has used drugs or alcohol in violation of the policy of the employer drawn from specific objective and articulate facts and reasonable inferences drawn from the facts in light of experience. Among other things, the facts and inferences may be based upon, but not limited to, the following:

a. Observable phenomena while at work such as direct observation of substance abuse or of the physical symptoms or manifestations or being impaired due to substance abuse.

b. Abnormal conduct or erratic behavior while at work or a significant deterioration in work performance.

c. A report of substance abuse provided by a reliable and credible source.

d. Evidence that an individual has tampered with any substance abuse test during his or her employment with the current employer.

e. Information that an employee has caused or contributed to an accident while at work.

f. Evidence that an employee has used, possessed, sold, solicited, or transferred drugs while working or while on the premises of the employer or while operating the employer's vehicle, machinery, or equipment.

(13) REHABILITATION PROGRAM. An established program capable of providing expert identification, assessment, and resolution of employee drug or alcohol abuse in a confidential and timely service. The service shall in all cases be provided by persons licensed or appropriately certified as health professionals to provide drug or alcohol rehabilitative services.

(14) SPECIMEN. Tissue, blood, breath, urine, or other product of the human body capable of revealing the presence of drugs or their metabolites or of alcohol.

(15) SUBSTANCE. Drugs or alcohol.

(16) SUBSTANCE ABUSE TEST OR TEST. Any chemical, biological, or physical instrument analysis administered for the purpose of determining the presence or absence of a drug or its metabolites or of alcohol.

**Sec. 25-5-332. Premium discount where drug-free workplace program implemented.** (a) If an employer implements a drug-free workplace program substantially in accordance with this article, the employer shall qualify for certification for a five percent premium discount under the employer's workers' compensation insurance policy.

(b) For each policy of workers' compensation insurance issued or renewed in the state on and after July 1, 1996, there shall be granted by the insurer a five percent reduction in the premium for the policy if the insured has been certified by the Department of Industrial Relations, Workers' Compensation Division, as having a drug-free workplace program which complies with the requirements of this article and has notified its insurer in writing of the certification.

(c)(1) The premium discount provided by this section shall be applied to an insured's policy of workers' compensation insurance pro rata as of the date the insured receives certification by the Department of Industrial Relations, Workers' Compensation Division, and shall continue for a period not to exceed four years. Notwithstanding the foregoing, an insurer shall not be required to credit the actual amount of the premium discount to the account of the insured until the final premium audit under the policy. Certification of an insured shall be required for each of the four years in which the premium discount is granted. Thereafter, any premium discount pursuant to this article shall be determined from the experience rating plan of the insured, or in the case of an insured not rated upon experience, as provided in subdivision (2).

(2) With respect to an insured which is not rated upon experience, any premium discount given an insured pursuant to this article after the initial four-year period provided in subdivision (1) shall be determined by the State Insurance Commissioner based upon data received from the rating and statistical organization designated by the commissioner pursuant to this article.

(d) The workers' compensation insurance policy of an insured shall be subject to an additional premium for the purposes of reimbursement of a previously granted premium discount and to cancellation in accordance with the policy if it is determined by the Department of Industrial Relations, Workers' Compensation Division, that the insured misrepresented the compliance of its drug-free workplace program.

(e) Each insurer shall make an annual report to the rating and statistical organization designated by the State Insurance Commissioner pursuant to this article illustrating the total dollar amount of drug-free workplace premium credit. Standard earned premium figures reported pursuant to this subsection on the aggregate calls for experience shall reflect the effects of the credits. The net standard premium shall then be the basis of any premium adjustment. The drug-free workplace credits shall be reported under a unique classification code or unit statistical reports submitted to the rating and statistical organization designated by the State Insurance Commissioner.

(f) The State Insurance Commissioner may promulgate rules and regulations necessary for the implementation and enforcement of this article.

**Sec. 25-5-333. Elements of program.** (a) A drug-free workplace program shall contain all the following elements:

(1) A written policy statement as provided in Section 25-5-334.

(2) Substance abuse testing as provided in Section 25-5-335.

(3) Resources of employee assistance providers maintained in accordance with Section 25-5-336.

(4) Employee education as provided in Section 25-5-337(a).

(5) Supervisor training in accordance with Section 25-5-337(b).

(b) In addition to the requirements of subsection (a), a drug-free workplace program shall be implemented in compliance with the confidentiality standards provided in Section 25-5-339.

**Sec. 25-5-334. Notice of testing; written policy statement.** (a) One time only, prior to testing, all employees and job applicants for employment shall be given a notice of testing. In addition, all employees shall be given a written policy statement from the employer which contains all of the following:

(1) A general statement of the employer's policy on employee substance abuse which shall identify:

a. The types of testing an employee or job applicant may be required to submit to, including reasonable suspicion or other basis used to determine when the testing will be required.

b. The actions the employer may take against an employee or job applicant on the basis of a positive confirmed test result.

(2) A statement advising an employee or job applicant of the existence of this article.

(3) A general statement concerning confidentiality.

(4) The consequences of refusing to submit to a drug test.

(5) A statement advising an employee of the Employee Assistance Program, if the employer offers the program, or advising the employee of the employer's resource file of assistance programs and other persons, entities, or organizations designed to assist employees with personal or behavioral problems.

(6) A statement that an employee or job applicant who receives a positive confirmed test result may contest or explain the result to the employer within five working days after written notification of the positive test result.

(7) A statement informing an employee of the provisions of the federal Drug-Free Workplace Act, if applicable to the employer.

(b) An employer not having a substance abuse testing program in effect on July 1, 1996, shall ensure that at least 60 days elapse between a general one-time notice to all employees that a substance abuse testing program is being implemented and the beginning of the actual testing. An employer having a substance abuse testing program in place prior to July 1, 1996, shall not be required to provide a 60-day notice period.

(c) An employer shall include notice of substance abuse testing on vacancy announcements for those positions for which testing is required. A notice of the employer's substance abuse testing policy shall also be posted in an appropriate and conspicuous location on the employer's premises, and copies of the policy shall be made available for inspection by the employees or job applicants of the employer during regular business hours in the employer's personnel office or other suitable locations. All testing conducted by an employer shall be in conformity with the standards and procedures established in this article and all applicable rules adopted by the State Department of Industrial Relations pursuant to this article. Notwithstanding the foregoing, an employer shall not have a legal duty under this article to request an employee or job applicant to undergo testing.

**Sec. 25-5-335. Types of tests; procedures for specimen collection and testing; laboratory; confirmation of tests.** (a) An employer is required to conduct the following types of tests in order to qualify for the workers' compensation insurance premium discounts provided under this article:

(1) An employer shall require job applicants to submit to a substance abuse test after extending an offer of employment. Limited testing of job applicants by an employer shall qualify under this article if the testing is conducted on the basis of reasonable classifications of job positions.

(2) An employer shall require an employee to submit to reasonable suspicion testing.

(3) An employer shall require an employee to submit to a substance abuse test if the test is conducted as part of a routinely scheduled employee fitness-for-duty medical examination that is part of the employer's established policy or that is scheduled routinely for all members of an employment classification or group.

(4) If the employee, in the course of employment, enters an employee assistance program or a rehabilitation program as the result of a positive test, the employer shall require the employee to submit to a substance abuse test as a follow-up to the program. Notwithstanding the foregoing, if an employee voluntarily entered the program, follow-up testing shall not be required. If follow-up testing is conducted, the frequency of the testing shall be at least once a year for a two-year period after completion of the program and advance notice of the testing date shall not be given to the employee.

(5) If the employee has caused or contributed to an on-the-job injury which resulted in a loss of work time, the employer shall require the employee to submit to a substance abuse test.

(b) Nothing in this article shall prohibit a private employer from conducting random testing or other lawful testing of employees.

(c) All specimen collection and testing under this article shall be performed in accordance with the following procedures:

(1) A specimen shall be collected with due regard to the privacy of the individual providing the specimen, and in a manner reasonably calculated to prevent substitution or contamination of the specimen.

(2) Specimen collection shall be documented, and the documentation procedures shall include all of the following:

a. Labeling of specimen containers so as to reasonably preclude the likelihood of erroneous identification of test results.

b. An opportunity for the employee or job applicant to record any information he or she considers relevant to the test, including identification of currently or recently used prescription or nonprescription medication or other relevant medical information. The providing of information shall not preclude the administration of the test, but shall be taken into account in interpreting any positive confirmed results.

(3) Specimen collection, storage, and transportation to the testing site shall be performed in a manner which reasonably precludes specimen contamination or adulteration.

(4) Each initial and confirmation test conducted under this article, not including the taking or collecting of a specimen to be tested, shall be conducted by a laboratory as described in subsection (d).

(5) A specimen for a test may be taken or collected by any of the following persons:

a. A physician, a physician's assistant, a registered professional nurse, a licensed practical nurse, a nurse practitioner, or a certified paramedic who is present at the scene of an accident for the purpose of rendering emergency medical service or treatment.

b. A qualified person certified or employed by a laboratory certified by the National Institute on Drug Abuse, the College of American Pathologists, or the Alabama Department of Human Resources.

(6) Within five working days after receipt of a positive confirmed test result from the laboratory, an employer shall inform the employee or job applicant in writing of the positive test result, the consequences of the results, and the options available to the employee or job applicant.

(7) The employer shall provide to the employee or job applicant, upon request, a copy of the test results.

(8) An initial test having a positive result shall be verified by a confirmation test.

(9) An employer who performs drug testing or specimen collection shall use chain of custody procedures to ensure proper record keeping, handling, labeling, and identification of all specimens to be tested.

(10) An employer shall pay the cost of all drug tests, initial and confirmation, which the employer requires of employees.

(11) An employee or job applicant shall pay the cost of any additional tests not required by the employer.

(12) If testing is conducted based on reasonable suspicion, the employer shall promptly detail in writing the circumstances which formed the basis of the determination that reasonable suspicion existed

to warrant the testing. A copy of this documentation shall be given to the employee upon request and the original documentation shall be kept confidential by the employer as provided in this article and retained by the employer for at least one year.

(d)(1) No laboratory may analyze initial or confirmation drug specimens unless:

a. The laboratory is approved by the National Institute on Drug Abuse or the College of American Pathologists.

b. The laboratory has written procedures to ensure the chain of custody.

c. The laboratory follows proper quality control procedures including, but not limited to:

1. The use of internal quality controls including the use of samples of known concentrations which are used to check the performance and calibration of testing equipment, and periodic use of blind samples for overall accuracy.

2. An internal review and certification process for drug test results, conducted by a person qualified to perform that function in the testing laboratory.

3. Security measures implemented by the testing laboratory to preclude adulteration of specimens and drug test results.

4. Other necessary and proper actions taken to ensure reliable and accurate drug test results.

(2)a. A laboratory shall disclose to the employer a written test result report within seven working days after receipt of the sample. All laboratory reports of a substance abuse test result shall, at a minimum, state all of the following:

1. The name and address of the laboratory which performed the test and the positive identification of the person tested.

2. Positive results on confirmation tests only, or negative results, as applicable.

3. A list of the drugs for which the drug analyses were conducted.

4. The type of tests conducted for both initial and confirmation tests and the minimum cut-off levels of the tests.

b. No report shall disclose the presence or absence of any drug other than a specific drug and its metabolites listed pursuant to this article.

(3) Laboratories shall provide technical assistance to the employer, employee, or job applicant for the purpose of interpreting any positive confirmed test results which could have been caused by prescription or nonprescription medication taken by the employee or job applicant.

(e) If an initial drug test is negative, the employer may seek a confirmation test. Only those laboratories described in subsection (d) shall conduct confirmation drug tests.

(f) All positive initial tests shall be confirmed using the gas chromatography/mass spectrometry (GC/MC) method or an equivalent or more accurate scientifically accepted methods approved by the National Institute on Drug Abuse as the technology becomes available in a cost-effective form.

**Sec. 25-5-336. Employee assistance program or resource file of employee assistance providers.** (a) If an employer has an employee assistance program, the employer shall inform the employee of the benefits and services of the employee assistance program. In addition, the employer shall provide the employee with notice of the policies and procedures regarding access to and utilization of the program.

(b) If an employer does not have an employee assistance program, the employer shall maintain a resource file of providers of other employee assistance including drug and alcohol abuse programs, mental health providers, and other persons, entities, or organizations available to assist employees with personal or behavioral problems and shall notify the employee of the availability of the resource file. In addition, the employer shall post in a conspicuous place a listing of providers or employee assistance in the area.

**Sec. 25-5-337. Semiannual education program; supervisor training.** (a) An employer shall provide all employees with a semiannual education program on substance abuse, in general, and its effects on the workplace, specifically. An education program for a minimum of one hour should include, but is not limited to, the following information:

(1) The explanation of the disease model of addiction for alcohol and drugs.

(2) The effects and dangers of the commonly abused substances in the workplace.

(3) The policies of the company and procedures regarding substance abuse in the workplace and how employees who wish to obtain substance abuse treatment can do so.

(b) In addition to the education program provided in subsection (a), an employer shall provide all supervisory personnel with a minimum of two hours of supervisor training, which includes, but is not limited to, the following information:

(1) How to recognize signs of employee substance abuse.

(2) How to document and collaborate signs of employee substance abuse.

(3) How to refer substance abusing employees to the proper treatment providers.

**Sec. 25-5-338. Construction of article.** (a) No physician-patient relationship is created between an employee or job applicant and an employer, medical review officer, or any person performing or evaluating a drug test solely by the establishment, implementation, or administration of a drug-testing program.

(b) Nothing in this article shall be construed to prevent an employer from establishing reasonable work rules related to employee possession, use, sale, or solicitation of drugs, including convictions for drug related offenses, and taking action based upon a violation of any of those rules.

(c) Nothing in this article shall be construed to operate retroactively, and nothing in this article shall abrogate the right of an employer under state or federal law to conduct drug tests, or implement employee drug-testing programs. Notwithstanding the foregoing, only those programs that meet the criteria outlined in this article qualify for reduced workers' compensation insurance premiums under this article.

(d) Nothing in this article shall be construed to prohibit an employer from conducting medical screening or other tests required, permitted, or not disallowed by any statute, rule, or regulation for the purpose of monitoring exposure of employees to toxic or other unhealthy materials in the workplace or in the performance of job responsibilities. The screening or tests shall be limited to the specific materials expressly identified in the statute, rule, or regulation, unless prior written consent of the employee is obtained for other tests.

(e) No cause of action shall arise in favor of any person based upon the failure of an employer to establish or conduct a program or policy for substance abuse testing.

**Sec. 25-5-339. Confidentiality of information.** (a) All information, interviews, reports, statements, memoranda, and test results, written or otherwise, received by the employer through a substance abuse testing program are confidential communications, but may be used or received in evidence, obtained in discovery, or disclosed in any civil or administrative proceeding, except as provided in subsection (c).

(b) Employers, laboratories, medical review officers, employee assistance programs, drug or alcohol rehabilitation programs, and their agents who receive or have access to information concerning test results shall keep all information confidential. Release of such information under any other circumstance shall be solely pursuant to a written consent form signed voluntarily by the person tested, unless the release is compelled by an agency of the state or a court of competent jurisdiction or unless deemed appropriate by a professional or occupational licensing board in a related disciplinary proceeding. The consent form shall contain at a minimum all of the following:

(1) The name of the person who is authorized to obtain the information.

(2) The purpose of the disclosure.

(3) The precise information to be disclosed.

(4) The duration of the consent.

(5) The signature of the person authorizing release of the information.

(c) Information on test results shall not be released or used in any criminal proceeding against the employee or job applicant. Information released contrary to this subsection shall be inadmissible as evidence in the criminal proceeding.

(d) Nothing contained in this article shall be construed to prohibit the employer or laboratory conducting a test from having access to employee test information when consulting with legal counsel when the information is relevant to its defense in a civil or administrative matter.

**Sec. 25-5-340. Department of Industrial Relations to perform administrative duties for certification of employers.** The Department of

Industrial Relations, Workers' Compensation Division, shall promulgate by rule or regulation procedures and forms for the certification of employers who establish and maintain a drug-free workplace which complies with this article. The department may charge a fee for the certification of a drug-free workplace program in an amount which shall approximate the administrative costs to the department of the certification. The certification fees shall be deposited in a revolving account to fund the administrative costs of certification and are hereby appropriated solely for that purpose. Certification of an employer shall be required for each year in which a premium discount is granted.

## P. Florida

*Fla. Stat. Ann. §§440.101–440.102 (1996 Supp.)*

**Sec. 440.101. Legislative intent; drug-free workplaces.** (1) It is the intent of the Legislature to promote drug-free workplaces in order that employers in the state be afforded the opportunity to maximize their levels of productivity, enhance their competitive positions in the marketplace, and reach their desired levels of success without experiencing the costs, delays, and tragedies associated with work-related accidents resulting from drug abuse by employees. It is further the intent of the Legislature that drug abuse be discouraged and that employees who choose to engage in drug abuse face the risk of unemployment and the forfeiture of workers' compensation benefits.

(2) If an employer implements a drug-free workplace program in accordance with s. 440.102 which includes notice, education, and procedural requirements for testing for drugs and alcohol pursuant to rules developed by the division, the employer may require the employee to submit to a test for the presence of drugs or alcohol and, if a drug or alcohol is found to be present in the employee's system at a level prescribed by rule adopted pursuant to this act, the employee may be terminated and forfeits his eligibility for medical and indemnity benefits. However, a drug-free workplace program must require the employer to notify all employees that it is a condition of employment for an employee to refrain from reporting to work or working with the presence of drugs or alcohol in his or her body and, if an injured employee refuses to submit to a test for drugs or alcohol, the employee forfeits eligibility for medical and indemnity benefits.

**Sec. 440.102. Drug-free workplace program requirements.** The following provisions apply to a drug-free workplace program implemented pursuant to rules adopted by the division:

**(1) Definitions.**—Except where the context otherwise requires, as used in this act:

(a) "Chain of custody" refers to the methodology of tracking specified materials or substances for the purpose of maintaining control and accountability from initial collection to final disposition for all such materials or substances and providing for accountability at each stage in handling, testing, and storing specimens and reporting test results.

(b) "Confirmation test," "confirmed test," or "confirmed drug test" means a second analytical procedure used to identify the presence of a specific drug or metabolite in a specimen, which test must be different in scientific principle from that of the initial test procedure and must be capable of providing requisite specificity, sensitivity, and quantitative accuracy.

(c) "Drug" means alcohol, including a distilled spirit, wine, a malt beverage, or an intoxicating liquor; an amphetamine; a cannabinoid; cocaine; phencyclidine (PCP); a hallucinogen; methaqualone; an opiate; a barbiturate; a benzodiazepine; a synthetic narcotic; a designer drug; or a metabolite of any of the substances listed in this paragraph. An employer may test an individual for any or all of such drugs.

(d) "Drug rehabilitation program" means a service provider, established pursuant to s. 397.311(28), that provides confidential, timely, and expert identification, assessment, and resolution of employee drug abuse.

(e) "Drug test" or "test" means any chemical, biological, or physical instrument analysis administered, by a laboratory certified by the United States Department of Health and Human Services or licensed by the Agency for Health Care Administration, for the purpose of determining the presence or absence of a drug or its metabolites.

(f) "Employee" means any person who works for salary, wages, or other remuneration for an employer.

(g) "Employee assistance program" means an established program capable of providing expert assessment of employee personal concerns; confidential and timely identification services with regard to employee drug abuse; referrals of employees for appropriate diagnosis, treatment, and assistance; and followup services for employees who participate in the program or require monitoring after returning to work. If, in addition to the above activities, an employee assistance program provides diagnostic and treatment services, these services shall in all cases be provided by service providers pursuant to s. 397.311(28).

(h) "Employer" means a person or entity that employs a person and that is covered by the Workers' Compensation Law.

(i) "Initial drug test" means a sensitive, rapid, and reliable procedure to identify negative and presumptive positive specimens, using an immunoassay procedure or an equivalent, or a more accurate scientifically accepted method approved by the United States Food and Drug Administration or the Agency for Health Care Administration as such more accurate technology becomes available in a cost-effective form.

(j) "Job applicant" means a person who has applied for a position with an employer and has been offered employment conditioned upon successfully passing a drug test, and may have begun work pending the results of the drug test. For a public employer, "job applicant" means only a person who has applied for a special-risk or safety-sensitive position.

(k) "Medical review officer" or "MRO" means a licensed physician, employed with or contracted with an employer, who has knowledge of substance abuse disorders, laboratory testing procedures, and chain of custody collection procedures; who verifies positive, confirmed test results; and who has the necessary medical training to interpret and evaluate an employee's positive test result in relation to the employee's medical history or any other relevant biomedical information.

(l) "Prescription or nonprescription medication" means a drug or medication obtained pursuant to a prescription as defined by s.893.02 or a medication that is authorized pursuant to federal or state law for general distribution and use without a prescription in the treatment of human diseases, ailments, or injuries.

(m) "Public employer" means any agency within state, county, or municipal government that employs individuals for a salary, wages, or other remuneration.

(n) "Reasonable-suspicion drug testing" means drug testing based on a belief that an employee is using or has used drugs in violation of the employer's policy drawn from specific objective and articulable facts and reasonable inferences drawn from those facts in light of experience. Among other things, such facts and inferences may be based upon:

1. Observable phenomena while at work, such as direct observation of drug use or of the physical symptoms or manifestations of being under the influence of a drug.

2. Abnormal conduct or erratic behavior while at work or a significant deterioration in work performance.

3. A report of drug use, provided by a reliable and credible source.

4. Evidence that an individual has tampered with a drug test during his employment with the current employer.

5. Information that an employee has caused, contributed to, or been involved in an accident while at work.

6. Evidence that an employee has used, possessed, sold, solicited, or transferred drugs while working or while on the employer's premises or while operating the employer's vehicle, machinery, or equipment.

(o) "Safety-sensitive position" means, with respect to a public employer, a position in which a drug impairment constitutes an immediate and direct threat to public health or safety, such as a position that requires the employee to carry a firearm, perform life-threatening procedures, work with confidential information or documents pertaining to criminal investigations, or work with controlled substances; a position subject to s. 110.1127; or a position in which a momentary lapse in attention could result in injury or death to another person.

(p) "Special-risk position" means, with respect to a public employer, a position that is required to be filled by a person who is certified under chapter 633 or chapter 943.

(q) "Specimen" means tissue, hair, or a product of the human body capable of revealing the presence of drugs or their metabolites, as approved by the United States Food and Drug Administration or the Agency for Health Care Administration.

**(2) Drug testing.**—An employer may test an employee or job applicant for any drug described in paragraph (1)(c). In order to qualify as having established a drug-free workplace program which affords an employer the ability to qualify for the discounts provided under s. 627.0915 and deny medical and indemnity benefits, under this chapter all drug testing conducted by employers shall be in conformity with the standards and procedures established in this section and all applicable rules adopted pursuant to this section. However, an employer does not have a legal duty under this section to request an employee or job applicant to undergo drug testing. If an employer fails to maintain a drug-free workplace program in accordance with the standards and procedures established in this section and in applicable rules, the employer shall not be eligible for discounts under s. 627.0915. All employers qualifying for and receiving discounts provided under s. 627.0915 must be reported annually by the insurer to the division.

**(3) Notice to employees and job applicants.**—

(a) One time only, prior to testing, an employer shall give all employees and job applicants for employment a written policy statement which contains:

1. A general statement of the employer's policy on employee drug use, which must identify:

a. The types of drug testing an employee or job applicant may be required to submit to, including reasonable-suspicion drug testing or drug testing conducted on any other basis.

b. The actions the employer may take against an employee or job applicant on the basis of a positive confirmed drug test result.

2. A statement advising the employee or job applicant of the existence of this section.

3. A general statement concerning confidentiality.

4. Procedures for employees and job applicants to confidentially report to a medical review officer the use of prescription or nonprescription medications to a medical review officer both before and after being tested.

5. A list of the most common medications, by brand name or common name, as applicable, as well as by chemical name, which may alter or affect a drug test. A list of such medications as developed by the Agency for Health Care Administration shall be available to employers through the Division of Workers' Compensation of the Department of Labor and Employment Security.

6. The consequences of refusing to submit to a drug test.

7. A representative sampling of names, addresses, and telephone numbers of employee assistance programs and local drug rehabilitation programs.

8. A statement that an employee or job applicant who receives a positive confirmed test result may contest or explain the result to the medical review officer within 5 working days after receiving

written notification of the test result; that if an employee's or job applicant's explanation or challenge is unsatisfactory to the medical review officer, the medical review officer shall report a positive test result back to the employer; and that a person may contest the drug test result pursuant to rules adopted by the Department of Labor and Employment Security.

9. A statement informing the employee or job applicant of his responsibility to notify the laboratory of any administrative or civil action brought pursuant to this section.

10. A list of all drugs for which the employer will test, described by brand name or common name, as applicable, as well as by chemical name.

11. A statement regarding any applicable collective bargaining agreement or contract and the right to appeal to the Public Employees Relations Commission or applicable court.

12. A statement notifying employees and job applicants of their right to consult with a medical review officer for technical information regarding prescription or nonprescription medication.

(b) An employer not having a drug-testing program shall ensure that at least 60 days elapse between a general one-time notice to all employees that a drug-testing program is being implemented and the beginning of actual drug testing. An employer having a drug-testing program in place prior to July 1, 1990, is not required to provide a 60-day notice period.

(c) An employer shall include notice of drug testing on vacancy announcements for positions for which drug testing is required. A notice of the employer's drug-testing policy must also be posted in an appropriate and conspicuous location on the employer's premises, and copies of the policy must be made available for inspection by the employees or job applicants of the employer during regular business hours in the employer's personnel office or other suitable locations.

**(4) Types of testing.—**

(a) An employer is required to conduct the following types of drug tests:

1. *Job applicant drug testing.*—An employer must require job applicants to submit to a drug test and may use a refusal to submit to a drug test or a positive confirmed drug test as a basis for refusing to hire a job applicant.

2. *Reasonable-suspicion drug testing.*—An employer must require an employee to submit to reasonable-suspicion drug testing.

3. *Routine fitness-for-duty drug testing.*—An employer must require an employee to submit to a drug test if the test is conducted as part of a routinely scheduled employee fitness-for-duty medical examination that is part of the employer's established policy or that is scheduled routinely for all members of an employment classification or group.

4. *Followup drug testing.*—If the employee in the course of

employment enters an employee assistance program for drug-related problems, or a drug rehabilitation program, the employer must require the employee to submit to a drug test as a followup to such program, unless the employee voluntarily entered the program. In those cases, the employer has the option to not require followup testing. If followup testing is required, it must be conducted at least once a year for a 2-year period after completion of the program. Advance notice of a followup testing date must not be given to the employee to be tested.

(b) This subsection does not preclude a private employer from conducting random testing, or any other lawful testing, of employees for drugs.

(c) Limited testing of applicants, only if it is based on a reasonable classification basis, is permissible in accordance with division rule.

**(5) Procedures and employee protection.**—All specimen collection and testing for drugs under this section shall be performed in accordance with the following procedures:

(a) A sample shall be collected with due regard to the privacy of the individual providing the sample, and in a manner reasonably calculated to prevent substitution or contamination of the sample.

(b) Specimen collection must be documented, and the documentation procedures shall include:

1. Labeling of specimen containers so as to reasonably preclude the likelihood of erroneous identification of test results.

2. A form for the employee or job applicant to provide any information he considers relevant to the test, including identification of currently or recently used prescription or nonprescription medication or other relevant medical information. The form must provide notice of the most common medications by brand name or common name, as applicable, as well as by chemical name, which may alter or affect a drug test. The providing of information shall not preclude the administration of the drug test, but shall be taken into account in interpreting any positive confirmed test result.

(c) Specimen collection, storage, and transportation to the testing site shall be performed in a manner that reasonably precludes contamination or adulteration of specimens.

(d) Each initial drug test and confirmation test conducted under this section, not including the taking or collecting of a specimen to be tested, shall be conducted by a licensed or certified laboratory as described in subsection (9).

(e) A specimen for a drug test may be taken or collected by any of the following persons:

1. A physician, a physician assistant, a registered professional nurse, a licensed practical nurse, or a nurse practitioner or a certified paramedic who is present at the scene of an accident for the purpose of rendering emergency medical service or treatment.

2. A qualified person employed by a licensed or certified laboratory as described in subsection (9).

(f) A person who collects or takes a specimen for a drug test shall collect an amount sufficient for two drug tests as determined by the Agency for Health Care Administration.

(g) Every specimen that produces a positive, confirmed test result shall be preserved by the licensed or certified laboratory that conducted the confirmation test for a period of at least 210 days after the result of the test was mailed or otherwise delivered to the medical review officer. However, if an employee or job applicant undertakes an administrative or legal challenge to the test result, the employee or job applicant shall notify the laboratory and the sample shall be retained by the laboratory until the case or administrative appeal is settled. During the 180-day period after written notification of a positive test result, the employee or job applicant who has provided the specimen shall be permitted by the employer to have a portion of the specimen retested, at the employee's or job applicant's expense, at another laboratory, licensed and approved by the Agency for Health Care Administration, chosen by the employee or job applicant. The second laboratory must test at equal or greater sensitivity for the drug in question as the first laboratory. The first laboratory that performed the test for the employer is responsible for the transfer of the portion of the specimen to be retested, and for the integrity of the chain of custody during such transfer.

(h) Within 5 working days after receipt of a positive confirmed test result from the medical review officer, an employer shall inform an employee or job applicant in writing of such positive test result, the consequences of such results, and the options available to the employee or job applicant. The employer shall provide to the employee or job applicant, upon request, a copy of the test results.

(i) Within 5 working days after receiving notice of a positive confirmed test result, an employee or job applicant may submit information to the employer explaining or contesting the test result, and explaining why the result does not constitute a violation of the employer's policy.

(j) The employee's or job applicant's explanation or challenge of the positive test result is unsatisfactory to the employer, a written explanation as to why the employee's or job applicant's explanation is unsatisfactory, along with the report of positive result, shall be provided by the employer to the employee or job applicant; and all such documentation shall be kept confidential by the employer pursuant to subsection (8) and shall be retained by the employer for at least 1 year.

(k) An employer may not discharge, discipline, refuse to hire, discriminate against, or request or require rehabilitation of an employee or job applicant on the sole basis of a positive test result that has not been verified by a confirmation test and by a medical review officer.

(l) An employer that performs drug testing or specimen collection shall use chain-of-custody procedures established by the Agency for Health Care Administration to ensure proper recordkeeping, handling, labeling, and identification of all specimens tested.

(m) An employer shall pay the cost of all drug tests, initial and confirmation, which the employer requires of employees. An employee or job applicant shall pay the costs of any additional drug tests not required by the employer.

(n) An employer shall not discharge, discipline, or discriminate against an employee solely upon the employee's voluntarily seeking treatment, while under the employ of the employer, for a drug-related problem if the employee has not previously tested positive for drug use, entered an employee assistance program for drug-related problems, or entered a drug rehabilitation program. Unless otherwise provided by a collective bargaining agreement, an employer may select the employee assistance program or drug rehabilitation program if the employer pays the cost of the employee's participation in the program.

(o) If drug testing is conducted based on reasonable suspicion, the employer shall promptly detail in writing the circumstances which formed the basis of the determination that reasonable suspicion existed to warrant the testing. A copy of this documentation shall be given to the employee upon request and the original documentation shall be kept confidential by the employer pursuant to subsection (8) and shall be retained by the employer for at least 1 year.

(p) All authorized remedial treatment, care, and attendance provided by a health care provider to an injured employee before medical and indemnity benefits are denied under this section must be paid for by the carrier or self-insurer. However, the carrier or self-insurer must have given reasonable notice to all affected health care providers that payment for treatment, care, and attendance provided to the employee after a future date certain will be denied. A health care provider, as defined in s. 440.13(1)(j), that refuses, without good cause, to continue treatment, care, and attendance before the provider receives notice of benefit denial commits a misdemeanor of the second degree, punishable as provided in s. 775.082 or s. 775.083.

**(6) Confirmation testing.—**

(a) If an initial drug test is negative, the employer may in its sole discretion seek a confirmation test.

(b) Only licensed or certified laboratories as described in subsection (9) may conduct confirmation drug tests.

(c) All positive initial tests shall be confirmed using gas chromatography/mass spectrometry (GC/MS) or an equivalent or more accurate scientifically accepted method approved by the Agency for Health Care Administration or the United States Food and Drug Administration as such technology becomes available in a cost-effective form.

(d) If an initial drug test of an employee or job applicant is confirmed as positive, the employer's medical review officer shall provide technical assistance to the employer and to the employee or job applicant for the purpose of interpreting the test result to determine whether the result could have been caused by prescription or nonprescription medication taken by the employee or job applicant.

**(7) Employer protection.**—

(a) An employee or job applicant whose drug test result is confirmed as positive in accordance with this section shall not, by virtue of the result alone, be deemed to have a "handicap" or "disability" as defined under federal, state, or local handicap and disability discrimination laws.

(b) An employer who discharges or disciplines an employee or refuses to hire a job applicant in compliance with this section is considered to have discharged, disciplined, or refused to hire for cause.

(c) No physician-patient relationship is created between an employee or job applicant and an employer or any person performing or evaluating a drug test, solely by the establishment, implementation, or administration of a drug-testing program.

(d) Nothing in this section shall be construed to prevent an employer from establishing reasonable work rules related to employee possession, use, sale, or solicitation of drugs, including convictions for drug-related offenses, and taking action based upon a violation of any of those rules.

(e) This section does not operate retroactively, and does not abrogate the right of an employer under state law to conduct drug tests, or implement employee drug-testing programs; however, only those programs that meet the criteria outlined in this section qualify for reduced rates under s. 627.0915.

(f) If an employee or job applicant refuses to submit to a drug test, the employer is not barred from discharging or disciplining the employee or from refusing to hire the job applicant. However, this paragraph does not abrogate the rights and remedies of the employee or job applicant as otherwise provided in this section.

(g) This section does not prohibit an employer from conducting medical screening or other tests required, permitted, or not disallowed by any statute, rule, or regulation for the purpose of monitoring exposure of employees to toxic or other unhealthy substances in the workplace or in the performance of job responsibilities. Such screening or testing is limited to the specific substances expressly identified in the applicable statute, rule, or regulation, unless prior written consent of the employee is obtained for other tests. Such screening or testing need not be in compliance with the rules adopted by the Department of Labor and Employment Security and the Agency for Health Care Administration under s. 112.0455. A public employer may, through the use of an unbiased selection procedure, conduct random drug tests of employees occupying safety-sensitive or special-risk positions if the testing is performed in accordance with drug-testing rules adopted by the Agency for Health Care Administration and the Department of Labor and Employment Security. If applicable, random drug testing must be specified in a collective bargaining agreement as negotiated by the appropriate certified bargaining agent before such testing is implemented.

(h) No cause of action shall arise in favor of any person based upon the failure of an employer to establish a program or policy for drug testing.

**(8) Confidentiality.—**

(a) Except as otherwise provided in this subsection, all information, interviews, reports, statements, memoranda, and drug test results, written or otherwise, received or produced as a result of a drug-testing program are confidential and exempt from the provisions of s. 119.07(1) and s. 24(a), Art. I of the State Constitution, and may not be used or received in evidence, obtained in discovery, or disclosed in any public or private proceedings, except in accordance with this section or in determining compensability under this chapter.

(b) Employers, laboratories, medical review officers, employee assistance programs, drug rehabilitation programs, and their agents may not release any information concerning drug test results obtained pursuant to this section without a written consent form signed voluntarily by the person tested, unless such release is compelled by a hearing officer or a court of competent jurisdiction pursuant to an appeal taken under this section or is deemed appropriate by a professional or occupational licensing board in a related disciplinary proceeding. The consent form must contain, at a minimum:

1. The name of the person who is authorized to obtain the information.
2. The purpose of the disclosure.
3. The precise information to be disclosed.
4. The duration of the consent.
5. The signature of the person authorizing release of the information.

(c) Information on drug test results shall not be used in any criminal proceeding against the employee or job applicant. Information released contrary to this section is inadmissible as evidence in any such criminal proceeding.

(d) This subsection does not prohibit an employer, agent of an employer, or laboratory conducting a drug test from having access to employee drug test information or using such information when consulting with legal counsel in connection with actions brought under or related to this section or when the information is relevant to its defense in a civil or administrative matter.

(e) The exemptions in this subsection are subject to the Open Government Sunset Review Act in accordance with s. 119.14.

**(9) Drug-testing standards for laboratories.—**

(a) A laboratory may not analyze initial or confirmation test specimens unless:

1. The laboratory is licensed and approved by the Agency for Health Care Administration using criteria established by the United States Department of Health and Human Services as guidelines for modeling the state drug-testing program pursuant to this section or

the laboratory is certified by the United States Department of Health and Human Services.

2. The laboratory has written procedures to ensure the chain of custody.

3. The laboratory follows proper quality control procedures, including, but not limited to:

a. The use of internal quality controls, including the use of samples of known concentrations which are used to check the performance and calibration of testing equipment, and periodic use of blind samples for overall accuracy.

b. An internal review and certification process for drug test results, conducted by a person qualified to perform that function in the testing laboratory.

c. Security measures implemented by the testing laboratory to preclude adulteration of specimens and drug test results.

d. Other necessary and proper actions taken to ensure reliable and accurate drug test results.

(b) A laboratory shall disclose to the medical review officer a written positive confirmed test result report within 7 working days after receipt of the sample. All laboratory reports of a drug test result must, at a minimum, state:

1. The name and address of the laboratory that performed the test and the positive identification of the person tested.

2. Positive results on confirmation tests only, or negative results, as applicable.

3. A list of the drugs for which the drug analyses were conducted.

4. The type of tests conducted for both initial tests and confirmation tests and the minimum cutoff levels of the tests.

5. Any correlation between medication reported by the employee or job applicant pursuant to subparagraph (5)(b)2. and a positive confirmed drug test result.

A report must not disclose the presence or absence of any drug other than a specific drug and its metabolites listed pursuant to this section.

(c) The laboratory shall submit to the Agency for Health Care Administration a monthly report with statistical information regarding the testing of employees and job applicants. The report must include information on the methods of analysis conducted, the drugs tested for, the number of positive and negative results for both initial tests and confirmation tests, and any other information deemed appropriate by the Agency for Health Care Administration. A monthly report must not identify specific employees or job applicants.

**(10) Rules.**—The Department of Labor and Employment Security shall adopt rules, using the rules adopted by the Agency for Health Care Administration pursuant to s. 112.0455 and criteria established by the United States Department of Health and Human Services as guidelines for modeling the state drug-testing program, concerning, but not limited to:

(a) Standards for licensing drug-testing laboratories and suspension and revocation of such licenses.

(b) Body specimens and minimum specimen amounts that are appropriate for drug testing.

(c) Methods of analysis and procedures to ensure reliable drug-testing results, including standards for initial tests and confirmation tests.

(d) Minimum cutoff detection levels for each drug or metabolites of such drug for the purposes of determining a positive test result.

(e) Chain-of-custody procedures to ensure proper identification, labeling, and handling of specimens tested.

(f) Retention, storage, and transportation procedures to ensure reliable results on confirmation tests and retests.

**(11) Public employees in safety-sensitive or special-risk positions.**—

(a) If an employee who is employed by a public employer in a safety-sensitive position enters an employee assistance program or drug rehabilitation program, the employer must assign the employee to a position other than a safety-sensitive position or, if such position is not available, place the employee on leave while the employee is participating in the program. However, the employee shall be permitted to use any accumulated annual leave credits before leave may be ordered without pay.

(b) An employee who is employed by a public employer in a special-risk position may be discharged or disciplined by a public employer for the first positive confirmed test result if the drug confirmed is an illicit drug under s. 893.03. A special-risk employee who is participating in an employee assistance program or drug rehabilitation program may not be allowed to continue to work in any special-risk or safety-sensitive position of the public employer, but may be assigned to a position other than a safety-sensitive position or placed on leave while the employee is participating in the program. However, the employee shall be permitted to use any accumulated annual leave credits before leave may be ordered without pay.

**(12) Denial of benefits.**—An employer shall deny an employee medical or indemnity benefits under this chapter, pursuant to this section.

**(13) Collective bargaining rights.**—This section does not eliminate the bargainable rights as provided in the collective bargaining process if applicable.

## Q. Montana

*The Montana statute on drug testing also deals with the use of polygraphy and is set out under that head.*

# ACCESS TO PERSONNEL RECORDS

## I. State Legislation

### Q. Wisconsin

*Wis. Stat. Ann. §103.13*

(1) In this section: (a) "Employe" has the meaning specified in s. 101.01(2)(a) and also includes former employes. (b) "Employer" has the meaning specified in s. 101.01(2)(b).

(2) Every employer shall, upon the request of an employe, which the employer may require the employe to make in writing, permit the employe to inspect any personnel documents which are used or which have been used in determining that employe's qualifications for employment, promotion, transfer, additional compensation, termination or other disciplinary action, and medical records, except as provided in subs. (5) and (6). An employe may request all or any part of his or her records, except as provided in sub. (6). The employer shall grant at least 2 requests by an employe in a calendar year, unless otherwise provided in a collective bargaining agreement, to inspect the employe's personnel records as provided in this section. The employer shall provide the employe with the opportunity to inspect the employe's personnel records within 7 working days after the employe makes the request for inspection. The inspection shall take place at a location reasonably near the employe's place of employment and during normal working hours. If the inspection during normal working hours would require an employe to take time off from work with that employer, the employer may provide some other reasonable time for the inspection. In any case, the employer may allow the inspection to take place at a time other than working hours or at a place other than where the records are maintained if that time or place would be more convenient for the employe.

(3) An employe who is involved in a current grievance against the employer may designate in writing a representative of the employe's union, collective bargaining unit or other designated representative to inspect the employe's personnel records which may have a bearing on the resolution of the grievance, except as provided in sub. (6). The employer shall allow such a designated representative to inspect that employee's personnel records in the same manner as provided under sub. (2).

(4) If the employe disagrees with any information contained in the personnel records, a removal or correction of that information may be mutu-

ally agreed upon by the employer and the employe. If an agreement cannot be reached, the employe may submit a written statement explaining the employe's position. The employer shall attach the employe's statement to the disputed portion of the personnel record. The employe's statement shall be included whenever that disputed portion of the personnel record is released to a 3rd party as long as the disputed record is a part of the file.

(5) The right of the employe or the employe's designated representative under sub. (3) to inspect personnel records under this section includes the right to inspect any personal medical records concerning the employe in the employer's files. If the employer believes that disclosure of an employe's medical records would have a detrimental effect on the employe, the employer may release the medical records to the employe's physician or through a physician designated by the employe, in which case the physician may release the medical records to the employe or to the employe's immediate family.

(6) The right of the employe or the employe's designated representative under sub. (3) to inspect his or her personnel records does not apply to: (a) Records relating to the investigation of possible criminal offenses committed by that employe. (b) Letters of reference for that employe. (c) Any portion of a test document, except that the employe may see a cumulative total test score for either a section of the test document or for the entire test document. (d) Materials used by the employer for staff management planning, including judgments or recommendations concerning future salary increases and other wage treatments, management bonus plans, promotions and job assignments or other comments or ratings used for the employer's planning purposes. (e) Information of a personal nature about a person other than the employe if disclosure of the information would constitute a clearly unwarranted invasion of the other person's privacy. (f) An employer who does not maintain any personnel records. (g) Records relevant to any other pending claim between the employer and the employee which may be discovered in a judicial proceeding. (Sec. 103.13(1) to (6), as amended by Ch. 339, L. 1980)

*Wis. Stat. Ann. §103.13(7)–(8)*

(7) The right of the employe or the employe's representative to inspect records includes the right to copy or receive a copy of records. The employer may charge a reasonable fee for providing copies of records, which may not exceed the actual cost of reproduction.

(8) Any employer who violates this section may be fined not less than $10 nor more than $100 for each violation. Each day of refusal or failure to comply with a duty under this section is a separable violation. (Secs. 103.13(7) and (8), as added by Ch. 164, L. 1982)

# JOB REFERENCE IMMUNITY

## I. State Legislation

### A. Alaska

*Alaska Stat. §09.65.160*

An employer who discloses information about the job performance of an employee or former employee to a prospective employer of the employee or former employee at the request of the prospective employer or the employee or former employee is presumed to be acting in good faith and, unless lack of good faith is shown by a preponderance of the evidence, may not be held liable for the disclosure or its consequences. For purposes of this section, the presumption of good faith is rebutted upon a showing that the employer or former employer (1) recklessly, knowingly, or with a malicious purpose disclosed false or deliberately misleading information; or (2) disclosed information in violation of a civil right of the employee or former employee that is protected under AS 18.80 or under comparable federal law. (Sec. 09.65.160, as amended by Ch. 12, L. 1993, effective Aug. 5, 1993)

### B. Arizona

*Ariz. Rev. Stat. Ann. §23-1362 (A) to (G)*

A. "Blacklist" means any understanding or agreement whereby the names of any person or persons, list of names, descriptions or other means of identification shall be spoken, written, printed or implied for the purpose of being communicated or transmitted between two or more employers of labor, their bosses, foremen, superintendents, managers, officers or other agents, whereby the laborer is prevented or prohibited from engaging in a useful occupation. Any understanding or agreement between employers, their bosses, foremen, superintendents, managers, officers or other agents, whether written or verbal; and it will make no difference whether the employers, their bosses, foremen, superintendents, managers, officers or other agents act individually or for some company, corporation, syndicate, partnership or society; and it will make no difference whether they are employed or acting as agents for one and the same or different companies, corporations, syndicates, partnerships or societies, it shall come within the meaning of this section.

B. It is not unlawful for a former employer to provide to a requesting employer, or agents acting in his behalf, information concerning a person's education, training, experience, qualifications and job performance to be used for the purpose of evaluating the person for employment. A copy of any written communication regarding employment must be sent by the employer providing the information to the former employee's last known address.

C. A former employer making a communication pursuant to subsection B is immune from civil liability unless the information communicated is false and defamatory and is acted on to the harm of the employee by the prospective employer and the communicator knows the information is false or acts with reckless disregard of the information's truth or falsity.

D. Communications concerning employees or prospective employees which are made by an employer or prospective employer, or by a labor organization, to a government body or agency and which are required by law or which are furnished pursuant to written rules or policies of the government body or agency are privileged.

E. An employer, including this state and its agencies, a labor organization or an individual is not civilly liable for privileged communications pursuant to subsection D.

F. In response to a request by another bank, savings and loan, or credit union, it is not unlawful for a bank, savings and loan, or a credit union to provide a written employment reference which advises of the applicants' involvement in a theft, embezzlement, misappropriation, or other defalcation which has been reported to federal authorities pursuant to federal banking guidelines. In order for the immunity provided in subsection C to apply, a copy of the written employment reference must be sent by the institution providing the reference to the last known address of the applicant in question.

G. No bank, savings and loan, or credit union shall be civilly liable for providing such an employment reference unless the information provided is false and the bank, savings and loan, or credit union providing the false information does so with knowledge and malice. (Sec. 23-1361(A) to (G), as amended by Ch. 278, L. 1987)

A. A person commits blacklisting if he knowingly exchanges, solicits or gives out any labor blacklist.

B. A person who commits blacklisting is guilty of a class 2 misdemeanor. (Sec. 23-1362(A) and (B), as added by Ch. 278, L. 1987)

## C. California

*Cal. Civil Code §47(c)*

A privileged publication or broadcast is one made:

* * *

(c) In a communication, without malice, to a person interested therein, (1) by one who is also interested, or (2) by one who stands in such a relation to the person interested as to afford a reasonable ground for supposing the motive for the communication to be innocent, or (3) who is requested by the person interested to give the information. This subdivision applies to and included a communication concerning the job performance or qualifications of an applicant for employment, based upon credible evidence, made without malice, by a current or former employer of the applicant to, and upon request of, the prospective employer. This subdivision shall not apply to a communication concerning the speech or activities of an applicant for employment if the speech or activities are constitutionally protected, or otherwise protected by Section 527.3 of the Code of Civil Procedure or any other provision of law. (Civil Code, Sec. 47(c), as amended by Ch. 364, L. 1994, effective Jan. 1, 1995)

## D. Florida

*Fla. Stat. Ann. §768.095*

An employer who discloses information about a former employee's job performance to a prospective employer of the former employee upon request of the prospective employer or of the former employee is presumed to be acting in good faith and, unless lack of good faith is shown by clear and convincing evidence, is immune from civil liability for such disclosure or its consequences. For purposes of this section, the presumption of good faith is rebutted upon a showing that the information disclosed by the former employer was knowingly false or deliberately misleading, was rendered with malicious purpose, or violated any civil right of the former employee protected under Ch. 760. (Sec. 768.095, as enacted by Ch. 165, L. 1991)

## E. Indiana

*Ind. Code §22-5-3-1*

**Sec. 22-5-3-1. Preventing discharged employee from obtaining work—Penalty.**—(a) A person who, after having discharged any employee from his service, prevents the discharged employee from obtaining employment with any other person commits a Class C infraction and is liable in penal damages to the discharged employee to be recovered by civil action; but this subsection does not prohibit a person from informing, in writing, any other person to whom the discharged employee has applied for employment a truthful statement of the reasons for the discharge.

(b) An employer that discloses information about a current or former employee is immune from civil liability for the disclosure and the consequences proximately caused by the disclosure, unless it is proven by a preponderance of the evidence that the information disclosed was known to be false at the time the disclosure was made.

(c) Upon written request by the prospective employee, the prospective employer will provide copies of any written communication from current or former employers that may affect the employee's possibility of employment with the prospective employer. The request must be received by the prospective employer not later than thirty (30) days after the application for employment is made to the prospective employer. (Sec. 22-5-3-1(a) to (c), as last amended by S.B. 85, L. 1995, effective July 1, 1995)

**Sec. 22-5-3-2. Damages for preventing employees from obtaining other work.**—If any railway company or any other company or partnership or corporation in this state shall authorize, allow or permit any of its or their agents to black-list any discharged employees, or attempt by words or writing, or any other means whatever, to prevent such discharged employee, or any employee who may have voluntarily left said company's service, from obtaining employment with any other person, or company, said company shall be liable to such employee in such sum as will fully compensate him, to which may be added exemplary damages. (Sec. 22-5-3-2)

. . . It shall be unlawful for any employment agency to circulate, publish, record or issue any report or information to cause the discharge of any person employed in any legitimate service. (Sec. 25-16-1-14, as amended by Ch. 25, L. 1927)

## F. Iowa

*Iowa Code Ann. §1*

(a) Unless otherwise provided by law, an employer, or an employer's designee, who discloses information about a current or former employee to a prospective employer of the employee shall be qualifiedly immune from civil liability.

(b) Unless otherwise provided by law, an employer who discloses information about a current or former employee to a prospective employer of the employee shall be absolutely immune from civil liability. The immunity applies only to disclosure of the following:

(1) Date of employment;
(2) pay level;
(3) job description and duties; and
(4) wage history.

(c) Unless otherwise provided by law, an employer who responds in writing to a written request concerning a current or former employee from a prospective employer of that employee shall be absolutely immune from civil liability for disclosure of the following information to which an employee may have access:

(1) Written employee evaluations which were conducted prior to the employee's separation from the employer and to which an employee shall be given a copy upon request; and

(2) whether the employee was voluntarily or involuntarily released from service and the reasons for the separation.

(d) This section shall apply to causes of action accruing on and after the effective date of this act. (Sec. 1(a) to (d), HB 2029, L. 1995, effective July 1, 1995)

## G. Louisiana

*La. Rev. Stat. Ann. §23:291*

A. Any employer that, upon request by a prospective employer or a current or former employee, provides accurate information about a current or former employee's job performance or reasons for separation, shall be immune from civil liability and other consequences of such disclosure provided such employer is not acting in bad faith. An employer shall be considered to be acting in bad faith only if it can be shown by a preponderance of the evidence that the information disclosed was knowingly false and deliberately misleading.

B. Any prospective employer who reasonably relies on information pertaining to an employee's job performance or reasons for separation, disclosed by a former employer, shall be immune from civil liability including liability for negligent hiring, negligent retention, and other causes of action related to the hiring of said employee, based upon such reasonable reliance, unless further investigation, including, but not limited to a criminal background check, is required by law.

C. As used in this Section, the following words and phrases shall have the meanings contained herein unless the context clearly requires otherwise:

(1) "Employer" means any person, firm, or corporation, including the state and its political subdivisions, and their agents, that has one or more employees, or individuals performing services under any contract of hire or service, expressed or implied, oral or written.

(2) "Employee" means any person, paid or unpaid, in the service of an employer.

(3) "Prospective employer" means any "employer," as defined herein, to which a prospective employee has made application, either oral or written, or forwarded a resume or other correspondence expressing an interest in employment.

(4) "Prospective employee" means any person who has made an application, either oral or written, or has sent a resume or other correspondence indicating an interest in employment.

(5) "Job performance" includes, but is not limited to, attendance, attitude, awards, demotions, duties, effort, evaluations, knowledge, skills, promotions, and disciplinary actions. (Sec. 23:291, as enacted by S. B. 688, L. 1995, effective Aug. 15, 1995)

## H. Maine

*Me. Rev. Stat. Ann. tit. 26, §598*

An employer who discloses information about a former employee's job performance or work record to a prospective employer is presumed to be acting in good faith and, unless lack of good faith is shown by clear and convincing evidence, is immune from civil liability for such disclosure or its consequences. Clear and convincing evidence of lack of good faith means evidence that clearly shows the knowing disclosure, with malicious intent, of false or deliberately misleading information. This section is supplemental to and not in derogation of any claims available to the former employee that exist under state law and any protections that are already afforded employers under state law. (Title 26, Sec. 598, as enacted by P.L. 335, L. 1995, effective Sept. 29, 1995)

## I. New Mexico

*N.M. Stat. Ann. §1*

When requested to provide a reference on a former or current employee, an employer acting in good faith is immune from liability for comments about the former employee's job performance. The immunity shall not apply when the reference information supplied was knowingly false or deliberately misleading, was rendered with malicious purpose or violated any civil rights of the former employee. (Sec. 1, Ch. 152, L. 1995, effective June 16, 1995)

## J. Tennessee

*Tenn. Code Ann. §1*

Any employer that, upon request by a prospective employer or a current or former employee, provides truthful, fair and unbiased information about a current or former employee's job performance is presumed to be acting in good faith and is granted a qualified immunity for the disclosure and the consequences of the disclosure. The presumption of good faith is rebuttable upon a showing by a preponderance of the evidence that the information disclosed was:

(1) Knowingly false;

(2) Deliberately misleading;

(3) Disclosed for a malicious purpose;

(4) Disclosed in reckless disregard for its falsity or defamatory nature; or

(5) Violative of the current or former employee's civil rights pursuant to current employment discrimination laws. (Sec. 1, S.B. 382, L. 1995, effective June 12, 1995)

## K. Utah

*Utah Code Ann. §34-42-1*

(1) An employer who in good faith provides information about the job performance, professional conduct, or evaluation of a former or current employee to a prospective employer of that employee, at the request of the prospective employer of that employee, may not be held civilly liable for the disclosure or the consequences of providing the information.

(2) There is a rebuttable presumption that an employer is acting in good faith when the employer provides information about the job performance, professional conduct, or evaluation of a former or current employee to a

prospective employer of that employee, at the request of the prospective employer of that employee.

(3) The presumption of good faith is rebuttable only upon showing by clear and convincing evidence that the employer disclosed the information with actual malice and with intent to mislead.

(4) For purposes of this section "actual malice" means knowledge that the information was false or reckless disregard of whether the information was false.

(5) This section does not alter any privileges that exist under common law. (Sec. 34-42-1, as enacted by SB 178, L. 1995, effective May 1, 1995)

# Part III

## Sample Business Forms[1]



[1]Forms are taken from material received from members of BNA's Personnel Policies Forum; some of these forms have been reprinted in *BNA's Policy and Practice Series.* They are designed to be used as "starting points" for the discussion and/or creation of a policy or procedure, and may be adapted to particular work environments. Users should be aware that the samples are illustrative only. Employers always should check with their legal counsel and review federal, state, and local laws or regulations (as well as conditions and terms of union contracts, if appropriate) before fashioning and putting into effect any guidance or procedure modeled after any of the samples contained herein. Many of these forms, and others, are available on disk in *BNA's Personnel Policy Writer* from BNA Plus, 1-800-452-7773.

## II. Privacy Policies and Personnel Files

### I. Employment File Confidentiality*

Information relative to an individual's employment at [Company Name] is confidential and only available to persons or organizations outside [Company Name] upon request of the employee, or, by court order. [Company Name] management personnel may review employee records when the information to be examined is needed in order to fulfill the manager's responsibilities. Employees may review information in their own personnel file pursuant to the Employee Access to Personnel Record Act.

*Reprinted from material received from members of BNA's Personnel Policies Forum.

## J. Employment Verification/References*

Any requests from third parties for references and verifications of employment must be referred to Human Resources. Employees receiving such requests should not respond to them, but should allow Human Resources to handle them. Dates of employment, title and salary is the only information (if any) which may be given out by Human Resources in response to such requests.

*Reprinted from material received from members of BNA's Personnel Policies Forum.

## K. Security/Safety*

### Confidential Information

Security is of paramount importance to [Company Name]. Our emphasis on security and the security measures we employ may be more stringent than you may have seen elsewhere. But there is good reason for this. It is a necessary part of our business. [Company Name], in the conduct of its business, has access to a great deal of confidential information, including the credit card information on millions of people. The Company must maintain the confidentiality of this sensitive information. Therefore, we need to restrict access to such information to only those employees with a need to have such access. Your cooperation is appreciated, but expected.

All information concerning any aspect of [Company Name] business, clients, members and employees is confidential and is not to be discussed with or revealed to any person except in the performance of your job duties. [Company Name] reserves the right to search any parcels (including, but not limited to, briefcases, handbags, purses, and lunch containers) upon entering or exiting the building. Employees are not permitted to bring any type of recording devices such as tape recorders or cameras to work. Due to the sensitive nature of [Company Name] business, surveillance cameras are located throughout the building.

[Company Name] maintains the policy that all paper must be shredded. Material to be shredded is to be placed only in black, unlined containers marked "Shred Only". All garbage (i.e., soda cans, candy/gum wrappers, tissues, etc.) must be placed in gray plastic-lined containers. If you have any doubt whether an item should be shredded or not, shred the item.

---

*Reprinted from material received from members of BNA's Personnel Policies Forum.

## L. Confidential Information and Practices*

Information concerning the condition and treatment of any patient is highly confidential and may not be discussed with anyone not responsible for the immediate care of the patient.

Any employee discussing confidential information with anyone other than those who are directly responsible for the patient's care, is subject to immediate discharge.

[Company Name] will collect and retain information about individuals as required for business, regulatory or legal reasons.

Employees may review their personnel record upon request and may, under appropriate circumstances, add a personal statement or additional information to these records. Review of records will take place in the presence of the employee's Supervisor or Human Resources personnel.

All requests from outside sources for employee information should be directed to the Human Resources Department. Employee consent for release of information will not be required in cases where release is necessitated by law or for verification of information currently on file. Access to personnel records will be limited to authorized persons for business purposes only. Personnel records are business records of [Company Name] and shall not be removed except upon appropriate authority.

---

*Reprinted from material received from members of BNA's Personnel Policies Forum.

## M. Use of Telephones*

Telephones in [Company Name] offices are for official use to serve the public. Unauthorized personal use is prohibited. Employees may use the phone at their work station ONLY WHEN NECESSARY (for example, to call home, doctor's office, etc.), *when necessary,* however excessive use is discouraged and limited so that *personal use shall be kept to a maximum of three (3) to five (5) minutes per call and no more than five (5) calls per day* (unless further restricted or otherwise prescribed by departmental rules) so that the lines of communication between work stations and the public may remain open. Nonbusiness long distance phone calls are prohibited.

Employees are assured and must expect no rights of privacy when using [Company Name] telephones. In certain departments where serving the public or customer service activities are vital to the public safety or welfare and in certain departments where it is vital telephone lines are kept open for public service, monitoring by the department via electronic means within the telephone system or otherwise may be utilized.

Violations of the above policy shall be grounds for disciplinary action.

---

*Reprinted from material received from members of BNA's Personnel Policies Forum.

## N. Employee Privacy Rights to Use of Property*

All [Company Name] property, including vehicles, equipment, supplies, desks, file cabinets, as well as offices, work sites, telephones, computers, word processors, or any other [Company Name] property, is subject to being searched or monitored during a duly-authorized investigation of theft, wrong doing or criminal activity.

Therefore, employees who have use of and access to such vehicles, equipment, desks, file cabinets, offices, work sites, telephones, computers, word processors, or any other [Company Name] property, shall not have any expectation of privacy in their use of same.

Lockers assigned to employees are subject to this rule. The [Company Name] will provide employees with locks, therefore there shall be no expectation of privacy in the use of said lockers.

---

*Reprinted from material received from members of BNA's Personnel Policies Forum.

## O. Exit Interview Questionnaire*

Every effort will be made to extend to all employees to participate in an Exit Interview. All information obtained is treated with due confidentiality and used to evaluate personnel oriented programs. This information is not permitted to reflect upon any individual.

### EXIT INTERVIEW QUESTIONNAIRE

We would appreciate your honest evaluation of your employment with [Company Name] and any information you are willing to share about your decision to terminate at this time. All responses will be treated as confidential. Please complete the following questionnaire and return to your supervisor or, if you prefer, directly to the HRD office, [Address].

1. Please place a "1" next to your primary reason for leaving [Company Name]. Indicate with an "x" any additional reasons.

   ____ Personal Reasons (C)
   ____ Medical Reasons (D)
   ____ Accepted Other Employment (G)
   ____ School Obligations (H)
   ____ Job Dissatisfaction (I)
   ____ Retirement (Q)
   ____ Other (please explain):

2. Please comment about your reason(s) for terminating employment.

______________________________________________
______________________________________________
______________________________________________
______________________________________________
______________________________________________
______________________________________________

3. What did you like most about working at [Company Name]?

______________________________________________
______________________________________________
______________________________________________
______________________________________________
______________________________________________
______________________________________________

---

*Reprinted from material received from members of BNA's Personnel Policies Forum.

4. What constructive comments do you have with respect to making [Company Name] a better place to work?

______________________________________________________________
______________________________________________________________
______________________________________________________________
______________________________________________________________
______________________________________________________________
______________________________________________________________

| ____________________ | ____________________ | ____________________ |
|---|---|---|
| Name | Center | Date |

Note to Supervisor: If employee is unavailable to complete this form, supervisor is to use Termination Codes found in the Supervisory Staff Handbook, 802-3, indicate on form that employee was unavailable, and submit to HRD with terminating paperwork.

## P. Personnel Records: Policy and Procedure*

PERSONNEL POLICY:

Personnel File
Each Center shall maintain a Personnel File for each employee containing employment application records, payroll and deduction authorizations, performance information, attendance records and other pertinent documents.

4.51

Medical Information
Any information related to an employee's medical condition or history, including any health examinations, shall be maintained in a Medical Only File separate from the employee's Personnel File.

4.52

Security of Personnel Records
All personnel records are confidential and shall be kept under adequate security. Personnel records are available for regulatory and legal investigation upon release by the center administrator. Without the written permission of the employee, only those persons in the employee's supervisory chain of command, the Quality Assurance Auditor, and the Vice President, Human Resource Development (HRD) shall have access to an employee's personnel records.

4.53

PROCEDURE:

I. All personnel records are confidential. "Adequate security" means that, when not in active use by the supervisor or other authorized personnel, files are to be maintained in a central, locked file. Personnel records are periodically audited by the Quality Control Officer. A written "Release of Information" must be secured from the employee for the contents of personnel records to be released to any other [Company Name] staff.

II. Each employing center and, at Central Services, the Human Resource Development department, will maintain personnel records including a Personnel File and a Medical Only File for each employee. A written record of items added and/or deleted from personnel records, including date, supervisor's initials, and name of document, is to be maintained for each file.

---

*Reprinted from material received from members of BNA's Personnel Policies Forum.

III. Personnel Files

A. Items maintained in the Personnel File include:

1. Employee Information Sheet (Form 406-A)
2. Employment Application and resume
3. Release of Information Authorization Form
4. Confirmation of Previous Employment Form
5. Applicant Reference Summary Form
6. Copy—New Employee Checklist
7. Employment Eligibility Verification Form (I-9)
8. *Copy—Personnel/Payroll Authorization(s) (PPA's)
9. *Copy—Withholding Forms
10. *Copy—Flexible Healthcare Enrollment Form
11. *Copy—Health Plan Enrollment Form
12. *Copy—Dental Care Network Enrollment Form
13. *Copy—Life Insurance Enrollment Form
14. *Copy—Supplemental Life Insurance and Long-Term Disability Insurance Acceptance/Waiver Form
15. *Copy—LTD Enrollment Card
16. *Copy—Pension/Savings Enrollment Forms
17. Signed Position Description
18. Employee Handbook Acknowledgement
19. Signed Performance Appraisals
20. Licenses as required
21. Police/child abuse checks as required (LIEN checks)
22. Driver's license/record documentation as required
23. Personal Leave Plan Request Forms (may be deleted after one year)
24. Personal Leave Plan Conversion Forms
25. Other information as required for center operation
26. Letters of commendation, etc.
27. Notices of corrective action/grievances and litigation
28. Leave of Absence Request Forms
29. Non-medical Workers' Compensation information
30. Unemployment Compensation information
31. *Copy—Employee Termination Checklist
32. Resignation letter or resignation form
33. Separation Review
34. Exit interview
35. *Copy—Benefit cancellation forms

*For positions reporting to Central Services, these documents are maintained in the payroll files.

B. In order to keep Central Service personnel records up to date, the supervisor/administrator is to process a PPA and applicable benefit enrollment/change forms in the event of changes in:

1. Name
2. Address
3. Telephone number
4. Marital status
5. Number and names of dependents
6. Beneficiary designations for any of the agency's insurance, pension, disability plans
7. Persons to be notified in case of emergency

When a change in number of dependents or marital status occurs, the employee should submit a new form W-4 for income tax withholding purposes to HRD.

C. All information in Personnel Files is to be kept confidential, and is to be disclosed within the agency only to persons within the employee's supervisory chain of command, and personnel office staff with a legitimate business need to know as determined by the Vice President, HRD.

D. Any employee may inspect his/her Personnel File up to four times a year. Employees desiring to inspect their Personnel Files should notify their supervisor or department head who will arrange a convenient time for the review. The employee has the right to inspect the files in private but with the administrator/supervisor present. Notes regarding documents may be made, and the employee may request copies of documents (at standard copy cost to employee), but no employee may delete documents except through the Problem Resolution Process (see Problem Resolution Procedure, 705). In case of disagreement, the employee may add a statement of disagreement to the file.

E. The center administrator and/or personnel officer is to conduct a periodic review of the information contained in each employee's Personnel File. Inappropriate information is to be destroyed.

F. At such time as an employee is promoted or transferred to another center or site, it is the responsibility of the former supervisor/administrator to forward the Personnel File and Medical Only File to the administrator of the new center.

G. Personnel Files are to be retained at the center for 10 years after employee termination, after which they are to be destroyed.

IV. Medical Only Files

A. In compliance with ADA and OSHA regulations the Medical Only File contains all medical/health information including the following:

1. All medical information, including physician's statements related to workers' compensation or Family/Medical LOA's; medical tests and physical examinations.
2. Training records pertaining to bloodborne pathogens including dates of sessions, summary of course content, name(s) and qualification(s) of trainers, and names and job titles of attendees.
3. Hepatitis B Consent/Waiver (Form 604-A).

B. Medical Only Files are confidential and must be kept separate from Personnel Files. They may be maintained in the same drawer as long as they are in a separate section of the drawer.

C. Medical Only Files must be retained for 30 years following termination.

V. Payroll Files

The Human Resource Development office at Central Services maintains all employee payroll/benefit records in Payroll Files. These are as follows:

A. Personnel/Payroll Authorizations—original

B. New employee checklist—original

C. Benefit enrollment forms—copies

D. Pension/Savings enrollment forms—copies

E. Garnishment information—original

F. Withholding information—original

G. Credit Union information—original

H. Miscellaneous deduction forms

I. Employee Termination Checklist—original

J. Benefit cancellation forms—copies

COMMENTARY:

An effective system for keeping records on job applicants, current employees, and former employees is essential to the proper administration of the center's personnel function. Likewise, the agency strongly believes in respect for the rights and dignity of each employee, and pledges to conduct its business so the privacy of all employees is protected.

Centers will only request, use, and retain written information about employees as required for business or legal reasons. Except for references required on a job application form, or recommendations from professional or institutional groups used to evaluate an employee's employability, any necessary personal information will be gained directly from the employee.

As personnel records contain the employee's work history, deletion of documents should be done with utmost care. Personal Leave requests and documentation of oral warnings—given the specified improvement in performance—may be deleted from Personnel Files after a period of 12 months. Documentation in the Medical Only File may not be deleted.

## Q. Personnel Reference Requests*

OPERATING POLICY:

Requests for references from persons or firms outside the agency concerning current, retired or terminated employees is to be limited to dates of employment, title or job position, and salary range for the position. If asked whether the supervisor would rehire, the answer is to be limited to a "yes" or "no."

Requests for other personnel information must be referred to the center administrator or the Vice President, HRD. No one else is authorized to release such information.

Written requests from bank and mortgage institutions, where employees are applying for mortgages/loans and the employees have given authorization for confirming employment and wage information will be honored by center administrators or the HRD/Payroll Departments.

PROCEDURE: (See also Confidentiality, 703)

I. Work References

A. An employee's most complete references are copies of formal performance appraisals. Upon termination, an employee may wish to have copies made of documents that will serve in the place of written references (see Personnel Records, 406).

B. Without a "Release of Information" form signed by the employee, the supervisor, center administrator or Vice President, HRD may only give the following information to prospective employers upon receiving a written or oral reference check:

1. Dates of employment
2. Position title and range of pay
3. A "Yes" or "No" answer to the question, "Would you rehire?"

C. Center administrators or the Vice President, HRD will honor written requests for work references that include a "Release of Information" form signed by the former employee. **This is not just a guideline, but an absolute requirement.**

Because of the possibility of litigious action, center administrators are discouraged from answering questions which are open-ended and/or require interpretation or opinion, and from responding to questions regarding reasons for termination.

*Reprinted from material received from members of BNA's Personnel Policies Forum.

If in doubt about responding to a reference request, contact the Vice President, HRD. This is especially true when the former employee has been guilty of unprofessional or abusive behavior.

II. Other Reference Requests

A. Center administrators or the Vice President, HRD may release the following information to law enforcement or judicial authorities without the written consent of the individual concerned:

1. Verification and dates of employment
2. Title or job position
3. Wage or salary information

B. Employees may authorize financial or mortgage institutions to confirm employment status and wage information. Center administrators and the HRD/payroll offices will honor *written* requests for such information.

COMMENTARY:

Reference check requests need to be answered by the center administrator where the former employee was employed. They should not be forwarded to HRD as the type of information requested is not centrally maintained.

## U. Smoking in the Workplace*

City of North Miami, Florida
Administrative Regulation 1-46
(Approved March 3, 1990)

**All Departments**

### TOBACCO OR TOBACCO PRODUCTS ABSTENTION AS PREEMPLOYMENT REQUIREMENT

### OBJECTIVE

To reduce the liability exposure to the City of North Miami, recognizing that:

1. The Surgeon General of the United States has declared that use of tobacco or tobacco products is a hazard to an individual's health; and
2. An employee's poor health, due to the continued use of tobacco or tobacco products, increases the loss experience of the group health insurance plans and group life insurance plans; and
3. Increases in loss experience result in increases in premium cost for insurance plans; and
4. Increases in premium costs for employees are borne by the General Fund and, subsequently, by the taxpayers of the City of North Miami.

To reduce the amount of lost productivity time due to absenteeism and on-the-job time lost to the City of North Miami, recognizing that:

1. An employee's poor health, due to the continued use of tobacco or tobacco products, increases the amount of lost work days and limited activity and thus reduces an employee's productivity; and
2. Decreases in employee productivity result in the decrease in efficiency of the City Government; and
3. Decreased efficiency is not an effective use of taxpayer's dollars.

### RESPONSIBILITIES

The Personnel Director is responsible for monitoring the compliance of the provisions of this Administrative Regulation.

### PROCEDURES

All applicants must be a non-user of tobacco or tobacco products for at least one year immediately preceding application, as evidenced by the sworn affidavit of the application.

---

*Reprinted from *BNA Policy and Practice Series—Sample Policies and Forms* 51:131 (1993).

CITY OF NORTH MIAMI, FLORIDA
DEPARTMENT OF PERSONNEL

**AFFIDAVIT**

I, ______________________, do hereby affirm that I have not been a user of tobacco or tobacco products for at least one (1) year immediately preceding my application for employment, in accordance with Administrative Regulation 1-46, City of North Miami.

Under the penalties of perjury, I declare that I have read the foregoing affidavit and that the facts stated in it are true.

DATED and SIGNED this ______ day of ______, 19 ______.

________________________________
Signature of Applicant

Sworn To and Subscribed Before Me.

___________________________ (Seal)
Notary Public

My Commission Expires:

________________________________

## VI. E-Mail and Other Electronic Systems

### A. Corporate E-Mail Policy*

#### (Northeastern Publishing Company)

This memorandum sets forth the Company's policy on access to and disclosure of electronic mail messages sent or received by Company employees who use the electronic mail system, and on the proper use of the electronic mail system generally. This policy may be changed at any time.

The electronic mail and other information systems of the Company are not to be used in a way that may be disruptive, offensive to others, or harmful to morale.

There is to be no display or transmission of sexually explicit images, messages, or cartoons, or any transmission or use of e-mail communications that contain ethnic slurs, racial epithets, or anything that may be construed as harassment or disparagement of others based on their race, national origin, sex, sexual orientation, age, disability, or religious or political beliefs. Violation of this policy will result in appropriate disciplinary action.

In general, employees should use the information systems for Company business only. The e-mail system should not be used to solicit or proselytize others for commercial ventures, religious or political causes, outside organizations, or other non-job-related solicitations.

All messages are Company records. The Company reserves the right to access and disclose all messages sent over its electronic mail system for any purpose.

For privacy reasons, employees should not attempt to gain access to another employee's personal file of e-mail messages without the latter's express permission. However, Company management reserves the right to enter an employee's e-mail files whenever there is a business need to do so.

---

*Reprinted from *BNA Policy and Practice Series—Sample Policies and Forms* 29:661 (1993).

## B. E-Mail: General Policies*

Certain Company locations have electronic mail and other forms of electronic communications software (all referred to as "e-mail") to enhance the quality of their internal business communication. E-mail may be used only for messages that relate to the business of the Company. Use for personal messages is not allowed.

Because e-mail is a business communications tool, all e-mail messages should be businesslike and professional in tone and content. Obscene, offensive, illegal, or unprofessional communication through e-mail is forbidden. This includes, but is not limited to:

- Obscene, profane, abusive, or threatening language or graphic representations;
- Statements or graphic representations that may be construed as discriminatory or offensive by reference to race, national origin, gender, religion, age, disability, sexual orientation, or other legally protected criteria;
- Reference to or discussion of any sexual acts, sexual relationships, dates, dating, or any personal relationships;
- Jokes of any nature;
- Communications that violate the personal privacy of, or are disrespectful of, any individual; and
- Communications in furtherance of any illegal activity, including, but not limited to, "football pools" and other forms of illegal gambling.

All messages, documents, data, and other materials that are entered in any Company owned computer or information system is confidential information that is the sole property of the Company and shall not be disclosed to any other person other than another employee for a need to-know basis only. In addition, no employee shall enter into another employee's computer files without specific authorization of his/her supervisor/manager.

All communications via e-mail are subject to access, review, and random audit by any officer of [Company Name] the Company's General Manager, or the designee of any of them subject only to considerations of corporate confidentiality. The Company reserves the right to disclose all messages sent over its electronic mail system for any purpose.

---

*Reprinted from material received from members of BNA's Personnel Policies Forum.

## C. Electronic Systems and Literature*

### Personal Telephone Calls/Facsimile Machines

At times it may be necessary and unavoidable for employees to make or receive personal local telephone calls, but their frequency and duration should be kept to a minimum. Employees should restrict any personal calls to their own time or after closing. Long distance calls can be made only with the permission of an employee's supervisor. Facsimile transmission (FAX) machines may not be used for personal use.

Our customers are entitled to the best in telephone service and our lines and staff should be kept available for them.

### Solicitation and the Distribution of Literature

Nonemployees may not solicit, proselytize, sell or distribute any items, printed material or literature for any purpose on our premises or on any property we own.

Employees may not solicit, proselytize, sell or distribute literature or printed material (except in connection with the United Way Campaign) during their working time or the working time of any employee approached, within our working areas.

### Electronic Mail System

This system has been installed to enhance interdepartmental communication and is to be used for legitimate business reasons only. From time to time this system may be monitored by [Company Name] to assure compliance.

The system may not be used:

- In ways that are disruptive, offensive to others or harmful to morale.
- For solicitation or proselytizing others for commercial purposes, religious or political causes, outside organizations or any other nonjob-related purpose.

---

*Reprinted from material received from members of BNA's Personnel Policies Forum.

## D. Policy Statement on Use of Electronic Systems*

[Company Name] electronic systems and equipment are an essential part of the resources necessary to conduct our business. As such, they are to be used to further [Company Name] business goals.

There is to be absolutely no use of systems for communications that contain ethnic slurs, racial epithets, or anything that may be construed as harassment or disparagement of others based on their race, national origin, sex, sexual orientation, age, disability, or religious beliefs. Moreover, it is never appropriate to use [Company Name] computers to transmit sexually explicit or otherwise offensive images, messages, or cartoons.

The disruption, expense, and harm to morale caused by violations of this policy require stringent enforcement. Anyone violating the above aspects of this policy will be subject to discipline, up to and including dismissal.

Finally, any information produced on [Company Name] systems is the property of [Company Name]. [Company Name] reserves the right to enter an employee's electronic system whenever there is a business need to do so.

*Reprinted from material received from members of BNA's Personnel Policies Forum.

## E. Policy on Use of the Internet and Other Electronic Communication*

### BACKGROUND

This policy is binding on [Company Name] employees whose Internet address ends in bna.com and/or who identify themselves as [Company Name] employees in electronic communications outside of [Company Name].

As a corporation, [Company Name] must be concerned about the accuracy, authenticity, and timeliness of information obtained electronically, about its legal obligations, and about the need to monitor and manage the use of the corporation's finite resources. As a result, [Company Name] reserves the right to access, review, copy, delete, and disclose all activities of all users of [Company Name] computer systems or the [Company Name] network, regardless of whether such users are authorized to use such systems or network for any purposes.

Users should be aware that [Company Name] and its systems personnel may, in the course of maintaining the system or network, access and review users' activities. If [Company Name] or its systems personnel discover possible evidence of illegal activity or activity that violates company policies or rules, [Company Name] may take appropriate disciplinary action, up to and including discharge and/or disclosure of evidence to law enforcement officials or other third parties.

### POLICY

Employees with management approval for access to the Internet, bulletin boards, and other electronic media may use these tools to meet their job responsibilities. Employees may perform such tasks as exploring source material, performing research, and using person-to-person e-mail under telephone guidelines. Employees *may not* engage in such direct communication as list services and chat groups without management approval.

1. **Employees have a responsibility to use their Internet access in an informed and responsible way,** conforming to network etiquette, customs, courtesies, and to corporate policy.
2. **Use exactly the same standards of care and professionalism used in any other business-related communications.**
   a. Be aware that every outgoing communication contains a [Company Name] signature and can be read by millions of people,

*Reprinted from material received from members of BNA's Personnel Policies Forum.

including our most important news sources, our biggest subscribers, and our competitors.

b. Consider an e-mail message as a postcard, rather than a sealed letter.
c. Apply the same standards of quality to Internet communications that apply to our published product.
d. Be aware of and respect all copyright and licensing agreements. Do not forward anyone's messages without permission.

3. **Before signing onto a list service, check the Library's database of list services** to which [Company Name] employees subscribe. Do not subscribe as an individual if someone at [Company Name] already subscribes to the listserv. If the listserv is not already available, notify the Library staff that you have subscribed, once you have management approval to do so.
4. **Whenever possible, employees should print out documents rather than download them** to conserve resources. Employees should not download anything for publication before ensuring (such as by checking with the Library) that the material is not already in house, that it is reliable and from the best source, and that it will be downloaded in an acceptable format.
5. **Use of the Internet is a privilege, not a right,** and the privilege may be revoked at any time for inappropriate conduct. Obvious examples of inappropriate conduct include:
   a. Use of the Internet or other electronic communications made available by [Company Name] for other than business reasons;
   b. Use of the Internet for unlawful or malicious activities;
   c. Use of abusive or objectionable language in either public or private messages;
   d. Misrepresentation of oneself or inappropriate representation of [Company Name];
   e. Activities that cause congestion and disruption of networks and systems;
   f. Activities that compromise [Company Name]'s position, reputation, or objectivity.
6. **There is to be absolutely no use of systems for communications that contain ethnic slurs, racial epithets, or anything that may be construed as harassment or disparagement** of others based on race, national origin, sex, sexual orientation, age, disability, or religious beliefs. Moreover, it is never appropriate to use [Company Name] computers to transmit sexually explicit or otherwise offensive images, messages, or cartoons.

# VII. Health-Related Policies

## A. Life-Threatening Illness*

The Company understands that an employee with a life-threatening disease, including, but not limited to, cancer, heart disease, and AIDS, may desire to continue working. This will be allowed if the employee is able to meet acceptable performance, and medical evidence establishes that the employee's condition is not a threat to others and that he/she can safely perform his/her job.

The Company, in consideration for an employee with a life-threatening disease, offers the following through the Human Resources Department:

- Management and employee education and information on terminal illness and specific life-threatening illnesses.
- Referral to agencies and organizations which offer supportive services for life-threatening illnesses.
- Benefit consultation to assist an employee in effectively managing health, leave, and other benefits.

An employee afflicted with a life-threatening disease is to be treated the same as any other employee.

When dealing with life-threatening illnesses, supervisors need to:

- Keep the condition CONFIDENTIAL and personal.
- Review with the employee the Company policy on such issues as employee assistance, leaves and disabilities, and other available benefits.
- Contact the Human Resources Department for information about a terminal illness, a specific life-threatening illness, or assistance in managing a situation that involves an employee with a life-threatening condition.
- Contact the Human Resources Department about concerns of possible contagiousness of an employee's illness.
- Contact the Human Resources Department to determine if a doctor's statement should be obtained for continued approval of the employee's presence at work posing no threat to the employee, coworker, or customer. The Company reserves the right to require a medical examination by a medical doctor appointed by the Company.

---

*Reprinted from material received from members of BNA's Personnel Policies Forum.

- Reasonable accommodations will be made within the essential functions of the job for an employee with a life-threatening illness.
- Be sensitive and responsive to coworker concerns and support employee education available through the Human Resources Department.
- Give no special consideration beyond *normal* transfer requests for employees feeling threatened by a coworker's life-threatening condition.
- Be sensitive to the fact that continued employment for an employee with a life-threatening illness may sometimes be therapeutically important to the remission or recovery process and may help to prolong the employee's life.
- Encourage employees to seek assistance from established community support groups for medical treatment and counseling services. Information on these can be obtained from the Human Resources Department.

The employee who is diagnosed with a life-threatening disease should:

- Inform his/her supervisor or the Human Resources Department of the condition as soon as possible.
- Provide the Human Resources Department with any pertinent medical information needed to make decisions regarding job assignments, ability to continue working, or ability to return to work. The Company may need a doctor's certification on the employee's ability to safely perform his/her duties.

## B. Life-Threatening Illnesses*

[Company Name] encourages employees with life-threatening illnesses to continue working as long as they are able providing their illness presents no threat to themselves, other employees, or persons the agency serves. [Company Name] shall attempt to make reasonable job accommodation when necessary to assist an employee with a life-threatening illness and reserves the right to reassign an employee with a life-threatening illness.

Providing the employee meets the benefit providers' requirements for coverage, employees with AIDS, cancer, or other life-threatening illnesses shall be entitled to the same benefits as other employees.

Medical conditions and records of all employees shall be maintained with the strictest confidentiality. Any employment decision regarding a person with a life-threatening illness shall be made by the Center administrator in consultation with the Vice President, HRD.

[Company Name] reserves the right to require any employee to undergo a medical examination by a doctor chosen by [Company Name] whenever there is question of an employee's fitness to work, or when there is reason to believe an employee's medical condition constitutes a threat to the safety or health of other employees or persons served by the agency.

---

*Reprinted from material received from members of BNA's Personnel Policies Forum.

**C. Policy on AIDS***

**TO:** All Employees

**FROM:** HR Department

***POLICY ON AIDS***

This is a restatement of a policy originally issued in 1986. It is [Company Name]'s policy to treat employees affected with AIDS in the same manner as employees affected with any other life-threatening illness.

Employees with AIDS or any other life-threatening illness, such as cancer or heart disease, are encouraged to continue in their normal pursuits, including work, as long as their condition allows them to perform in an acceptable manner. [Company Name] will make reasonable accommodations (including rearranged and/or part-time duties) to enable ill employees to continue working to the extent possible. [Company Name]'s group health insurance program, COPE, sick leave, annual leave, personal leave, leave without pay, and long-term disability benefits are also available to assist ill employees.

Employee health information is personal and confidential. The Human Resources Department takes steps in its procedures to protect information about employees' health. Managers and other employees also have a responsibility to respect and maintain the confidentiality of such information.

Managers and coworkers are expected to treat ill employees the same as they would all other employees, while at the same time being sensitive to their conditions. Serious illness could afflict any of us or any of our families, and we would all want to be treated with the same consideration. There are no recorded cases of AIDS being spread through casual contact, including the workplace.

Employees with concerns about AIDS in the workplace are encouraged to contact Human Resources and our employee assistance plan, COPE, for information about AIDS and the services and resources available to help themselves and others.

---

*Reprinted from material received from members of BNA's Personnel Policies Forum.

## A. Application for Employment*

Mead

# Application for Employment

An equal opportunity employer

## Personal

Name—First | Middle | Last

Present Address | City | County | State | How long?

Zip Code | Telephone | Social Security Number

Prior Address | City | County | State | How long?

Are you eligible to work in the United States? Yes/No
Proof of eligibility will be required before you can be employed.

What date are you available for employment?

Have you ever applied for a position at Mead? | Location | When?

Are you presently on layoff or leave of absence from any other company?

Have you ever been convicted of a felony? (Conviction will not necessarily disqualify you from employment)

If yes, explain.

Do you have any commitments or agreements with another employer that might affect your employment with Mead?

If yes, explain.

## Education

| | | | | | | |
|---|---|---|---|---|---|---|
| Elementary School City/State | Circle grade completed: 1 2 3 4 5 6 7 8 | | | | | |
| High School City/State | Circle grade completed: 1 2 3 4 | | | | Did you graduate? | |
| College(s) City/State | Date from | Date to | Date graduated | Date degree received/expected | Average grade | Course major/field |
| | | | | | | |
| | | | | | | |
| | | | | | | |
| Other job-related educational institutions, licenses, certifications, etc. | | | | | | |
| | | | | | | |

The Mead Corporation will not discriminate against any employee or applicant for employment because of age (as defined by applicable law), religion, sex, race, color, national origin, or because they are handicapped, a disabled veteran or a Vietnam era veteran. Answers to application questions will be utilized for applicable, job related information only.

*Reprinted from *BNA Policy and Practice Series—Sample Policies and Forms* 5:107 (1993).

## Employment data

Give past employment record as completely as possible starting with latest employer (include military service).

| Employer name, address, and telephone no. | Date from | Date to | Salary–Monthly earnings | Nature of work/title |
|---|---|---|---|---|
| | Full-time | Part-time | Name of your immediate supervisor | Reason for leaving |

| Employer name, address, and telephone no. | Date from | Date to | Salary–Monthly earnings | Nature of work/title |
|---|---|---|---|---|
| | Full-time | Part-time | Name of your immediate supervisor | Reason for leaving |

| Employer name, address, and telephone no. | Date from | Date to | Salary–Monthly earnings | Nature of work/title |
|---|---|---|---|---|
| | Full-time | Part-time | Name of your immediate supervisor | Reason for leaving |

| Employer name, address and telephone no. | Date from | Date to | Salary–Monthly earnings | Nature of work/title |
|---|---|---|---|---|
| | Full-time | Part-time | Name of your immediate supervisor | Reason for leaving |

| Employer name, address, and telephone no. | Date from | Date to | Salary–Monthly earnings | Nature of work/title |
|---|---|---|---|---|
| | Full-time | Part-time | Name of your immediate supervisor | Reason for leaving |

| Employer name, address, and telephone no. | Date from | Date to | Salary–Monthly earnings | Nature of work/title |
|---|---|---|---|---|
| | Full-time | Part-time | Name of your immediate supervisor | Reason for leaving |

## References

List at least two responsible adults who have knowledge of your work ethic, experience, and ability. (Do not include relatives, former or present employers, or fellow employees.)

| Name | Address | Telephone No. | Occupation |
|---|---|---|---|
| | | | |
| | | | |

## Work preferences

Answer only the questions that apply to you and the position for which you are applying.

What type of employment do you want? ____ Full-time ____ Part-time ____ Summer

For what type of position are you applying?

Are you willing to travel? What percent of the time?

Are you willing to relocate? What is your minimum salary requirement?

Will you work shifts?

Word processing experience? Please describe:

Computer experience? Please describe:

**As an applicant for employment with the Mead Corporation, I understand the following:**

- This application will remain on active file for 60 days. If I am hired within this period, this form will be transferred to my individual personnel file.
- If I am not hired within 60 days, this application is no longer active and I will need to reapply for employment if I wish to be considered for a job with Mead.
- **Any misrepresentation or falsification of information or significant omissions will be cause for rejection of my application or for subsequent discipline up to and including my dismissal from employment if discovered at a later date.**
- I am required to submit to a prehiring physical examination in order for Mead to determine my physical ability to perform my job.
- **My employment is contingent upon the results of a drug screening analysis for substance abuse. The results of such analysis may be grounds for disqualifying me or terminating my employment.**
- If my application for employment is accepted, the effective date of my employment shall be the time I actually begin to work. If I am employed, I agree to comply with and be bound by the safety and health rules and regulations, and rules of conduct of the Company together with the obligations set forth in the Company's Invention's Agreement, if applicable.
- **My employment is not guaranteed for any term, and my employment may be terminated by the Company or myself at any time and for any reason. No management official is authorized to make any oral assurance or promise of continued employment.**
- All information (including information on any accompanying resume) is subject to verification.
- **I authorize and consent to my current and prior employers, educational institutions, and persons or organizations named in this application (or accompanying resume) to release any information to Mead that may be required to make an employment decision.**

Signature ____________________

Date ____________________

(See reverse side for personal data release.)

Mead

## Authorization for release of personal data

I, the undersigned, hereby authorize and request any present or former employer, educational institution, law enforcement agency, financial institution, or other persons having personal knowledge about me to furnish the Mead Corporation, and/or its agents, with any and all information in their possession regarding me, in connection with an application for or retention of employment. Further, I hereby release from liability and hold harmless all persons and corporations supplying this information to the Mead Corporation and/or its agents. A photocopy of this authorization is as effective as the original.

Signed ______________________________

Date ______________________________

## B. Application for Employment*

### *Application for Employment*

Last Name

First Name

Middle Initial

CSC

**Computer Sciences Corporation**
**An Equal Opportunity Employer**

**Return To:**

*Reprinted from *BNA Policy and Practice Series—Sample Policies and Forms* 5:121 (1993).

# Application for Employment

***Instructions:*** Please print and complete all questions. Include any supplemental information that you feel would be helpful in our consideration of your qualifications. If you need additional space for your responses below, use the comments/other accomplishments section of this questionnaire, or use additional sheets.

***Applicant Identification***

Date: ____/____/____

Name: ______________________________ (Last, First, Middle)

How were you referred to CSC: ____________________

Address: ______________________________ (Street)

______________________________ (City, State, Zip Code)

Social Security No.: ______-______-______

Phone: (____)__________ Home (____)__________ Business

Are you over 18 years of age?: ❑ Yes ❑ No

Are there any other names under which your employment or educational records, references, and other information in the application may be verified?

If so, list: ______________________________

If hired, can you furnish proof that you are either a U.S. Citizen, or otherwise legally permitted to work in the United States?: ❑ Yes ❑ No

***Type of Employment Desired***

Preferred Position: ______________________________

Date you could begin working: ____/____/____

Preferred Location: ______________________________

Would you consider relocation?: ❑ No ❑ Yes

Preferred Shift: __________ Desired Starting Salary: __________

If yes, state geographic preference: ____________________

Applying for: ❑ Full Time ❑ Part Time / Hours: ______ ❑ Temporary

***Education:*** Your educational record will be considered only to the extent that it is relevant to the job sought.

| Name & Address of High School: | Academic Majors: | GPA/Rank in Class: |
|---|---|---|
| | | |

| Name & Address of Colleges or Trade Schools (Including Military Schools): | From (Mo./Yr.): | To (Mo./Yr.): | Academic Majors: | GPA: | Degree: | Date (Mo./Yr.): |
|---|---|---|---|---|---|---|
| | | | | | | |
| | | | | | | |
| | | | | | | |

***Extracurricular Activities and Scholarships:*** List those extracurricular activities and scholarships which you believe are related to the position for which you are applying. (You may exclude those that may suggest race, religious creed, sex, marital status, age, color, national origin, or physical handicap.)

______________________________

______________________________

***Proficiencies:*** If you are applying for a position in which computer skills or secretarial/clerical skills are relevant, please answer the following (if you have questions about whether such skills are relevant, ask CSC's Human Resources Representative).

List all makes and models of computers and operating systems with which you have had operations experience:

______________________________

______________________________

List all computer languages with which you have had experience:

______________________________

______________________________

List all data processing, telecommunications, or office equipment on which you are proficient:

______________________________

______________________________

______________________________

Shorthand method: ____________________

Shorthand speed: ________ w.p.m. Typing speed: ________ w.p.m.

***United States Military Service:*** If you obtained any experience or skills while in military service that relate to the job for which you are applying, please describe the nature of your duties that led to the experience.

______________________________

______________________________

***Instructions:*** Please print and list every position that you have held for the past ten years starting with your present or most recent position. (Account for all periods of unemployment.) If you require additional space to detail your employment history, please request an Employment History Attachment from CSC's Human Resources Representative.

---

***Employment Background:*** Present or most recent position.

Employer: ______

Address: ______ (Street, City, State, Zip Code)

Name and Title of Supervisor: ______

Your current or last position and duties: ______

______

Your starting position and duties: ______

______

Other compensation (give detail on current commissions, incentives, bonuses, etc.): ______

______

May we contact your present employer for a reference?
☐ Yes ☐ No

Phone: (____)______

Employed From (Mo./Yr.): ______

Employed To (Mo./Yr.): ______

Total Months: ______

Starting Base Pay: ______

Ending Base Pay: ______

Reason for leaving: ______

______

---

***Employment Background:*** Previous position.

Employer: ______

Address: ______ (Street, City, State, Zip Code)

Name and Title of Supervisor: ______

Your last position and duties: ______

______

Your starting position and duties: ______

Other compensation (give detail): ______

Phone: (____)______

Employed From (Mo./Yr.): ______

Employed To (Mo./Yr.): ______

Total Months: ______

Starting Base Pay: ______

Ending Base Pay: ______

Reason for leaving: ______

______

---

***Employment Background:*** Previous position.

Employer: ______

Address: ______ (Street, City, State, Zip Code)

Name and Title of Supervisor: ______

Your last position and duties: ______

______

Your starting position and duties: ______

Other compensation (give detail): ______

Phone: (____)______

Employed From (Mo./Yr.): ______

Employed To (Mo./Yr.): ______

Total Months: ______

Starting Base Pay: ______

Ending Base Pay: ______

Reason for leaving: ______

______

---

***Comments and Accomplishments:*** Explain below, or on another sheet, your primary area of specialization. If applying for administrative, management or technical positions, outline all programs designed or implemented. If applying for marketing/sales, detail your sales experience, the kind of products sold and the customers serviced. Note any other details which should be considered in reviewing your qualifications including professional affiliations, honors and awards, theses, publications, patents, etc. (You may exclude professional affiliations which may suggest the race, religious creed, sex, marital status, age, color, national origin, or physical handicap of its members.)

______

______

---

***References:*** List individuals who can attest to your professional abilities/work accomplishments. (Do not include individuals listed in Employment Background section.)

| Name: | Address: | Business Phone: | Reference's Position or Relationship to you: |
|---|---|---|---|
| ______ | ______ | (___)______ | ______ |
| ______ | ______ | (___)______ | ______ |
| ______ | ______ | (___)______ | ______ |

***Security Information***

Have you ever been employed by Computer Sciences Corporation or subsidiary companies? ❑ No ❑ Yes If yes, give dates and location:

Do you have relatives employed by Computer Sciences Corporation or subsidiary companies? ❑ No ❑ Yes If yes, give name(s) and location(s):

Do you presently hold a security clearance? ❑ No ❑ Yes If yes, state level: ________________

Have you ever held a security clearance? ❑ No ❑ Yes If yes, state level and dates held:

Have you ever been denied a security clearance or had one revoked or suspended? ❑ No ❑ Yes If yes, explain: ________________

Have you ever been convicted of a felony (using your current name or under any other name)? ❑ No ❑ Yes

If yes, explain below (Include full name under which you were convicted. Conviction will not necessarily disqualify an applicant from employment.):

________________________________________

________________________________________

***EEO Policy***

CSC maintains a policy of non-discrimination for all employees and applicants in every facet of the company's operations. In compliance with federal and state laws, CSC hires, trains, and promotes all qualified employees without unlawful discrimination on the basis of race, color, sex, age, religious creed, marital status, citizenship, national origin, physical or mental handicap. This policy also applies to disabled veterans and veterans of the Vietnam Era.

If you wish to discuss CSC's Affirmative Action/Equal Employment Opportunity Policies and Programs, please contact a CSC Human Resources Representative.

***Certifications***

I understand and agree that this application is not a contract and that acceptance of employment is not a contract of employment for a specified term. I understand and agree that I may resign my employment with CSC at any time for any reason, and that my employment may be terminated at the will of CSC at any time for any reason. I also understand that any handbooks, manuals, policies, and procedures maintained by CSC are not contractual in nature and may be amended or abolished at the sole discretion of CSC at any time.

Further, should I become an employee of CSC, I will adhere to CSC's Code of Ethics and Standards of Conduct, will report all suspected violations of law related thereto, and will conduct the company's business in a strictly ethical and legal manner. Furthermore, I acknowledge that CSC has established a Drug-FreeAwareness Program and that as a condition of beginning employment with CSC I will be required to successfully complete a drug screening test for the presence of controlled substances. Should I become an employee of CSC, I will abide by the terms of CSC's Drug Abuse Policy and related management instructions. I will, in addition, obey all of the laws of the United States and of all localities, states, and nations where CSC does business or seeks to do business.

Persons employed by CSC have access to confidential information regarding various phases of Company business. Therefore, the Company follows the usual practice of requiring new employees at the time of employment to sign an agreement for assignment of inventions and covenant against disclosure. I understand that I must sign such agreement as a condition of employment. (Please ask a CSC Human Resources Representative for a copy.)

Pursuant to the Immigration Reform and Control Act, CSC will employ only those individuals who are eligible to work in the United States. Accordingly, upon hiring, all new employees will be required to demonstrate their eligibility to work in the United States. Failure to do so will result in termination or revocation of the offer of employment.

In addition, present and former employees of the Department of Defense affected by Section 931 of the Defense Acquisition Improvement Act of 1986 will be expected to provide approval documentation from their designated DoD Agency Ethics Official prior to the effective date of their employment with CSC.

I certify that I have read, understand and will adhere to the aforementioned statements.

I also certify that the information furnished in this application and any supporting documents is true and complete to the best of my knowledge and belief and I understand that any misrepresentation or omission of material fact on this or any other record submitted pertinent to employment will constitute grounds for immediate dismissal.

Signature of Applicant: ________________________ Date: ____/____/____

For information regarding employment with CSC, write or phone the Human Resources Manager at any of the following locations:

**Corporate Office**

2100 East Grand Avenue
El Segundo, California 90245
Phone: 213.615.0311

**Systems Group**

**Applied Technology Division**
6565 Arlington Boulevard
Falls Church, Virginia 22046
Phone: 703.237.2000

**Integrated Systems Division**
P.O. Box N
304 West Route 38
Moorestown, New Jersey 08057
Phone: 609.234.1100

**Network Systems Division**
3001 Centreville Road
Herndon, Virginia 22071
Phone: 703.471.3112

**Systems Engineering Division**
3160 Fairview Park Drive
Falls Church, Virginia 22042
Phone: 703.876.1000

**System Sciences Division**
4061 Powder Mill Road
Calverton, Maryland 20705
Phone: 301.572.3700

**Industry Services Group**

**CSC Credit Services, Inc.**
*A Subsidiary of*
*Computer Sciences Corporation*
652 E. North Belt, Suite 400
Houston, Texas 77060
Phone: 713.878.4913

**CSC Healthcare Services**
34505 West Twelve Mile Road, Suite 300
Farmington Hills, Michigan 48331
Phone: 313.553.0900

**CSC Tacs Division**
4515 Eagle Rock Boulevard
Los Angeles, California 90041
Phone: 213.258.8227

**Health and Administrative Services Division**
4601 Presidents Drive
Lanham, Maryland 20706
Phone: 301.306.9100

**CSC Consulting**

**Communications & Integration Services Division**
371 Hoes Lane
Piscataway, New Jersey 08854
Phone: 201.981.9119

**CSC Partners, Inc.**
*A Subsidiary of*
*Computer Sciences Corporation*
1 University Office Park
Waltham, Massachusetts 02154
Phone: 617.647.0116

**Index Group, Inc.**
*A Subsidiary of*
*Computer Sciences Corporation*
5 Cambridge Center
Cambridge, Massachusetts 02142
Phone: 617.492.1500

**Cleveland Consulting Associates, Inc.**
*A Subsidiary of*
*Computer Sciences Corporation*
300 Monarch Center
5885 Landerbrook Drive
Cleveland, Ohio 44124
Phone: 216.449.3600

C 01173 (11/90)

## *Application for Employment*
### *Employment History Attachment*

---

***Employment Background:*** Previous position.

Employer: ______________________________

Address: ______________________________ Phone: (____)____________
Street City State Zip Code

Name and Title of Supervisor: ______________________________ Employed From (Mo./Yr.): ________

Your last position and duties: ______________________________ Employed To (Mo./Yr.): ________

______________________________ Total Months: ________

______________________________ Starting Base Pay: ________

Your starting position and duties: ______________________________ Ending Base Pay: ________

______________________________ Reason for leaving: ________

Other compensation (give detail on current commissions, incentives, bonuses, etc.): ______________________________

______________________________

---

***Employment Background:*** Previous position.

Employer: ______________________________

Address: ______________________________ Phone: (____)____________
Street City State Zip Code

Name and Title of Supervisor: ______________________________ Employed From (Mo./Yr.): ________

Your last position and duties: ______________________________ Employed To (Mo./Yr.): ________

______________________________ Total Months: ________

______________________________ Starting Base Pay: ________

Your starting position and duties: ______________________________ Ending Base Pay: ________

______________________________ Reason for leaving: ________

Other compensation (give detail on current commissions, incentives, bonuses, etc.): ______________________________

______________________________

---

***Employment Background:*** Previous position.

Employer: ______________________________

Address: ______________________________ Phone: (____)____________
Street City State Zip Code

Name and Title of Supervisor: ______________________________ Employed From (Mo./Yr.): ________

Your last position and duties: ______________________________ Employed To (Mo./Yr.): ________

______________________________ Total Months: ________

______________________________ Starting Base Pay: ________

Your starting position and duties: ______________________________ Ending Base Pay: ________

______________________________ Reason for leaving: ________

Other compensation (give detail on current commissions, incentives, bonuses, etc.): ______________________________

______________________________

C 011738 (1/88)

# *Application for Employment*
## *Special Considerations Attachment*

**Special Consideration for Individuals with Handicaps, Vietnam Era Veterans and Special Disabled Veterans**

***Applicant Identification***

Name: ______________________________ Date: ____ ____ ____
Last First Middle

Preferred Position: ______________________________ Social Security Number: ______-____-________

CSC is a Government contractor subject to Section 503 of the Rehabilitation Act of 1973 and Section 2012 of the Vietnam Era Veterans Readjustment Assistance Act of 1974. These laws require Government contractors to take Affirmative Action to employ and advance in employment qualified persons with a handicap and qualified Vietnam Era veterans.

If you are an Individual with a Handicap, a Vietnam Era Veteran, or a Special Disabled Veteran and would like to be considered under our Affirmative Action Program, we invite you to share this information with us, strictly on a voluntary basis.

Refusal to provide information will not subject you to discharge or any adverse treatment.

The information will be kept confidential, except that which is necessary to ensure proper placement and to accommodate a disability or handicap that you have identified.

If you choose not to be included in CSC's Affirmative Action Program for Individuals with Handicaps, Vietnam Era Veterans and Special Disabled Veterans, please sign your name and mark your choice in the Election of Affirmative Action section below.

***Affirmative Action Catagory***

To be included in our Affirmative Action Program, please indicate how you would like to be identified:

❑ Individual with a Handicap

Check no more than one: ❑ (1) Veteran ❑ (2) Vietnam Era Veteran ❑ (3) Special Disabled Veteran ❑ (4) Special Disabled Vietnam Veteran

***Vietnam Era Veteran***

If you have chosen to be identified as a Vietnam Era Veteran, please complete this section:

Dates of active duty: From: ___/___/___ To: ___/___/___ Type of discharge or release: ______________________

***Physical Accommodations***

Do you have any physical condition or handicap that may limit your ability to perform the job for which you are applying or which may endanger the health and safety of others?

❑ Yes ❑ No

If the answer to the above question is yes, please describe any special methods, skills, or procedures you would use to perform the job.

______________________________

______________________________

______________________________

______________________________

You can assist us by describing the accommodations that we could make to enable you to perform the job properly and safely. Accommodations include special equipment, changes in the physical layout of the work environment, and the elimination of certain duties related to the job.

______________________________

______________________________

______________________________

______________________________

***Election of Affirmative Action***

Indicate your choice to be included in CSC's Handicapped, Vietnam Era Veterans and Special Disabled Veterans Affirmative Action Program:

❑ Yes, I choose to be included. ❑ No, I do not choose to be included.

Signature of Applicant: ______________________________ Date: ____/____/____

C 01173A (1/89)

## C. Application for Employment*

**PLEASE READ FIRST**

Thank you for your interest in employment with Public Service Electric and Gas Company. The application you submit will be reviewed and, if, based upon the information you have supplied, there is a need to schedule you for a pre-placement testing session and/or a personal interview, you will be contacted by phone or mail. If, however, we are unable to consider your application, you will receive no further notice. Applications are valid for only one year and if you have not received a response during this time period, you are welcome to re-apply. Due to the large volume of employment inquiries received, we regret that we are unable to provide a more personal response to your application.

**PLEASE FOLLOW THESE INSTRUCTIONS TO COMPLETE THIS APPLICATION**

1. Please complete the application in neat, legible handwriting using blue or black ink.

2. The application must be complete with date of employment, job titles, reasons for leaving, schools you attended, current mailing address, telephone number(s) and social security number.

3. Complete addresses must be provided for schools and previous employers. A complete mailing address includes street number, street, city, state, and zip code.

4. Your application must be completed providing all information required to evaluate your job application.

5. Complete application front and back.

AN INCOMPLETE APPLICATION WILL NOT BE CONSIDERED.

*Reprinted from *BNA Policy and Practice Series—Sample Policies and Forms* 5:131 (1993).

PSE&G is an EQUAL OPPORTUNITY EMPLOYER. To help us comply with government record keeping requirements, we would appreciate your completing the following form. You are not required to provide this information. If you choose not to provide the information, your decision will not affect your application.

This data will be kept confidential, and only be used in accordance with applicable state and federal laws and regulations.

(Please Print) Date ________________

Name ______________________________________________________________
Last First Middle

SS#_____/_____/______ ________Male ________Female

Race/Ethnicity Data (Check (✔) only one)

| | | |
|---|---|---|
| White | 1___ | A person having origins in any of the original peoples of Europe, North Africa, or the Middle East. |
| Black | 2___ | A person having origins in any of the Black racial groups of Africa. |
| Asian or Pacific Island | 3___ | A person having origins in any of the original or peoples of the Far East, Southeast Asia, the Indian subcontinent, or the Pacific Islands. This area includes, for example, China, India, Japan, Korea, the Phillipine Islands and Samoa. |
| American Indian or Alaskan Native | 4___ | A person having origins in any of the original peoples of North America, who maintains cultural identification through tribal affiliation or community recognition. |
| Hispanic | 5___ | A person of Mexican, Puerto Rican, Cuban, Central or South American, or other Spanish culture or origin, regardless of race. |

# Application For Employment

*PLEASE **PRINT** AND ANSWER **ALL** QUESTIONS ON **BOTH** SIDES OF THIS APPLICATION.*
*SHADED AREAS FOR COMPANY USE ONLY.*

| | | | | | | |
|---|---|---|---|---|---|---|
| DATE<br>MO. DAY YEAR | FULL NAME LAST | | FIRST | MIDDLE | | SALARY DESIRED |
| PRESENT STREET ADDRESS | CITY | | COUNTY | STATE | ZIP CODE | HOW LONG? |
| PREVIOUS STREET ADDRESS | CITY | | COUNTY | STATE | ZIP CODE | DATE OF BIRTH IF UNDER 18 |
| SOCIAL SECURITY NO. | TELEPHONE (9 A.M.-4 P.M.) | | HOME TELEPHONE | | | |
| ARE YOU CURRENTLY AUTHORIZED TO ACCEPT FULLTIME EMPLOYMENT IN THE UNITED STATES? [ ] YES [ ] NO | | | | | | |

# Education

| EDUCATION | NAME OF SCHOOL | ADDRESS OF SCHOOL | COURSE | GRADE COM-PLETED | CERTI-FICATE |
|---|---|---|---|---|---|
| (05) HIGH SCHOOL<br>(04) ATTENDING<br>(03) SOME | | | | | DIPLOMA<br>☐ NO<br>☐ YES |
| VOCATIONAL<br>(07) OR<br>TRADE SCHOOL | | | | | CERT.<br>☐ NO<br>☐ YES |
| COLLEGE<br>(06) PARTIAL<br>(08) ATTENDING<br>(09) ASSOC. DEG<br>(10) BACHELOR'S DEGREE | | | | | DEGREE<br>☐ NO<br>☐ YES |
| OTHER | | | | | |

PROFESSIONAL LICENSES AND AFFILIATIONS

DO YOU HAVE ANY SPECIAL TRAINING? [ ] WORD PROCESSING ________________ EQUIP.

[ ] TYPING ________________ EST. WPM [ ] P.C. ________________ SOFTWARE ________________

[ ] STENO ________________ EST. WPM [ ] OTHER ________________

ARE YOU WILLING TO WORK OVERTIME AS REQUIRED? ☐ NO ☐ YES

ARE YOU WILLING TO WORK DAY, EVENING OR NIGHT SHIFTS? ☐ NO ☐ YES

ARE YOU WILLING TO WORK SATURDAYS, SUNDAYS AND HOLIDAYS? ☐ NO ☐ YES

DO YOU HAVE A VALID DRIVER'S LICENSE? [ ] YES [ ] NO (REQUIRED FOR SOME POSITIONS) STATE
DO YOU HAVE A COMMERCIAL D.L.? [ ] YES [ ] NO

HAS YOUR DRIVER'S LICENSE BEEN SUSPENDED OR REVOKED IN THE LAST TWO YEARS? ☐ NO ☐ YES - EXPLAIN IN DETAIL AS TO DATE, PLACE, VIOLATION AND DISPOSITION ON NEXT LINE

HAVE YOU EVER BEEN CONVICTED OF ANY VIOLATION OF LAW OR UNIFORM CODE OF MILITARY JUSTICE OTHER THAN MINOR TRAFFIC VIOLATIONS? ☐ NO ☐ YES - EXPLAIN FULLY
(AN AFFIRMATIVE ANSWER IS NOT AN AUTOMATIC BAR TO EMPLOYMENT)

HAVE YOU EVER BEEN EMPLOYED BY PSE&G? ☐ NO ☐ YES - WHEN:
(AN AFFIRMATIVE ANSWER IS NOT AN AUTOMATIC BAR TO EMPLOYMENT.) WHERE:

HAVE YOU EVER BEEN INTERVIEWED FOR A POSITION AT PSE&G BEFORE? ☐ NO ☐ YES - WHEN:
(AN AFFIRMATIVE ANSWER IS NOT AN AUTOMATIC BAR TO EMPLOYMENT.) WHERE:

HAVE YOU EVER BEEN TESTED FOR A POSITION AT PSE&G BEFORE? ☐ NO ☐ YES - WHEN:
(AN AFFIRMATIVE ANSWER IS NOT AN AUTOMATIC BAR TO EMPLOYMENT.) WHERE:

**PREVIOUS EMPLOYMENT** LIST PRESENT OR MOST RECENT JOB FIRST (INCLUDE ANY MILITARY SERVICE)

| FROM | | TO | | EMPLOYER | PRINCIPAL DUTIES | TITLE |
|---|---|---|---|---|---|---|
| MO. | YR. | MO. | YR. | ADDRESS | SUPERVISOR'S NAME AND TITLE | |
| SALARY | | | | REASON FOR LEAVING | YOUR NAME AT TIME (IF DIFFERENT) | |
| FROM | | TO | | EMPLOYER | PRINCIPAL DUTIES | TITLE |
| MO. | YR. | MO. | YR. | ADDRESS | SUPERVISOR'S NAME AND TITLE | |
| SALARY | | | | REASON FOR LEAVING | YOUR NAME AT TIME (IF DIFFERENT) | |
| FROM | | TO | | EMPLOYER | PRINCIPAL DUTIES | TITLE |
| MO. | YR. | MO. | YR. | ADDRESS | SUPERVISOR'S NAME AND TITLE | |
| SALARY | | | | REASON FOR LEAVING | YOUR NAME AT TIME (IF DIFFERENT) | |
| FROM | | TO | | EMPLOYER | PRINCIPAL DUTIES | TITLE |
| MO. | YR. | MO. | YR. | ADDRESS | SUPERVISOR'S NAME AND TITLE | |
| SALARY | | | | REASON FOR LEAVING | YOUR NAME AT TIME (IF DIFFERENT) | |

HAVE YOU EVER BEEN DISCHARGED OR ASKED TO RESIGN FROM ANY POSITION? ☐ NO ☐ YES IF YES - EXPLAIN FULLY (AN AFFIRMATIVE ANSWER IS NOT AN AUTOMATIC BAR TO EMPLOYMENT)

HOW DID YOU BECOME INTERESTED IN WORKING FOR PUBLIC SERVICE?

AT WHAT LOCATION ARE YOU COMPLETING THIS APPLICATION?

In processing this application PSE&G may obtain an "investigative consumer report" as defined in the Fair Credit Reporting Act contained in Title VI of Public Law 95-508. Further information on the nature and scope of such a report, if one is made, is available to you upon written request.

**AFFIRMATION:**

I understand that any employment offer will be contingent upon the successful completion of a pre-placement medical examination and background investigation. As a part of PSE&G's requirement for a work force free from the influence of foreign chemical substances, the pre-placement medical examination will include a definitive analysis of a freshly voided urine specimen for the presence of commonly abused drugs including marijuana.

To the best of my knowledge all information on this application is true and correct. I understand any false statements, representations, or failure to disclose pertinent information is sufficient cause for dismissal from the Company's service if hired.

I understand that an offer of employment is not an employment contract and that I or the Company may terminate an employment relationship at any time.

X______________________________
SIGNATURE OF APPLICANT

**AUTHORIZATION:**

I authorize and consent to every person, firm, company, corporation, governmental agency, court, association, school, college, university or institution having control of any documents, records and other information pertaining to me, to furnish such information, upon request by Public Service Electric & Gas Company. I do also authorize the National Personnel Records Center and/or Army/Navy/Marine/Air Force/Coast Guard or their reserve components, to release information in their files about me to the Company or its authorized agents.

This "Authorization" will serve as a release of any and all information and for this purpose a photo copy shall be considered an original and valid.

I have read and fully understand the contents of this "Authorization".

X______________________________
SIGNATURE OF APPLICANT DATE

**PLEASE DO NOT WRITE BELOW THIS LINE — COMPANY USE ONLY**

## D. Interview Guidelines*

**INTERVIEW GUIDELINES**
**(Northeastern Communications Company)**

| PROCEDURE MANUAL | Section **PERSONNEL** |
|---|---|
| | Subject **INTERVIEW GUIDELINES** |

1.0 INTRODUCTION

These guidelines were prepared to help facilitate successful compliance with both federal and state laws. Federal and state laws and regulations applying to Equal Employment Opportunity prohibit inquiries that express, directly or indirectly, any preference, limitation, specification, or discrimination as to race, religion, color, national origin, sex, age, disability, or marital status. The guidelines presented here will be an aid for anyone who interviews, hires, or reviews current employees with regard to recruiting, transferring, or promoting.

2.0 INTERVIEW GUIDELINES

| Subject | You MAY Ask* | You MAY NOT Ask* |
|---|---|---|
| Race or Color | | About complexion or color of skin. |
| Religion or Creed | | About an applicant's religious denomination, religious affiliation, church, synagogue, parish, pastor, rabbi, or religious holidays observed. (An applicant may not be told: "This is a Catholic, Jewish, or Protestant organization.") |

| Date | CONFIDENTIAL | PAGE 1 of 6 |
|---|---|---|

*Reprinted from *BNA Policy and Practice Series—Sample Policies and Forms* 5:301 (1993).

HIRING AND EMPLOYMENT

| PROCEDURE MANUAL | Section **PERSONNEL** |
| --- | --- |
| | Subject **INTERVIEW GUIDELINES** |

| Subject | You MAY Ask* | You MAY NOT Ask* |
| --- | --- | --- |
| National Origin | | About an applicant's lineage, ancestry, national origin, descent, parentage, or nationality. About the nationality of applicant's parents or spouse. (What is your mother tongue?) |
| Sex | | A preemployment inquiry as to sex on an application. |
| Marital Status | | Are you married? Where does your spouse work? What are the ages of your children, if any? |
| Age | Are you between 18 and 65 years of age? If not, state your age. | How old are your? What is your date of birth? |

| Date | CONFIDENTIAL | PAGE 2 of 6 |
| --- | --- | --- |

| PROCEDURE MANUAL | Section **PERSONNEL** |
| --- | --- |
| | Subject **INTERVIEW GUIDELINES** |

| Subject | You MAY Ask* | You MAY NOT Ask* |
| --- | --- | --- |
| Disability | Do you have any impairments, physical or mental, which would interfere with your ability to perform the job for which you have applied? If there are any positions or types of positions for which you should not be considered or job duties you can not perform because of a physical handicap, please explain. | Do you have a disability? Have you even been treated for any of the following diseases? Has any member of your family ever had any of the following diseases? |
| Name | Have you ever worked for this company under a different name? Is any additional information relative to change of name, use of an assumed name, or nickname necessary to enable a check on your record? If yes, explain. | Original name of an applicant whose name has been changed by court order or otherwise. Maiden name of a married woman. If you have ever worked under another name, state name and dates. |
| Address or Duration of Residence | Applicant's place of residence. How long have you been a resident of this state or city? | |

| Date | CONFIDENTIAL | PAGE 3 of 6 |
| --- | --- | --- |

| PROCEDURE MANUAL | Section<br>**PERSONNEL** |
|---|---|
| | Subject<br>**INTERVIEW GUIDELINES** |

| Subject | You MAY Ask* | You MAY NOT Ask* |
|---|---|---|
| Birthplace | | Birthplace of applicant. Birthplace of applicant's parents, spouse, or other close relatives. |
| Photograph | | An applicant to affix a photograph to the application or other employment form at any time before hiring or at applicant's option. |
| Citizenship | Are you a citizen of the United States? If you are not a citizen of the United States, do you intent to become a citizen of the United States? If you are not a United States citizen, have you the legal right to remain permanently in the United States? Where you ever interned or arrested as an enemy alien? | Of what country are you a citizen? Whether an applicant is a naturalized or a native-born citizen; the date when the applicant acquired citizenship. That the applicant produce naturalization papers or first papers. Whether applicant's parents or spouse is naturalized or native-born citizen of the United States; the date when such parents or spouse acquired citizenship. |

| Date | CONFIDENTIAL | PAGE<br>4 of 6 |
|---|---|---|

| PROCEDURE MANUAL | Section<br>**PERSONNEL** |
|---|---|
| | Subject<br>**INTERVIEW GUIDELINES** |

| Subject | You MAY Ask* | You MAY NOT Ask* |
|---|---|---|
| Language | What foreign language(s) do you read fluently? Write fluently? Speak Fluently? | How applicant acquired ability to read, write, or speak a foreign language. |
| Education | About the academic, vocational, or professional education of an applicant and the public and private schools attended. | |
| Experience | About the aplicant's work experience. Inquire into countries applicant has visited. | |
| Character | Have you ever been convicted of any crime? If so, when, where, and what was disposition of offense? | Have you ever been arrested? (An employer's use of individual's arrest record to deny employment would, in the absence of business necessity, constitute a violation of the human rights law.) |
| Relatives | What are the names of any relatives already employed by this company? | Names, addresses, ages, number, or other information concerning applicant's children or other relatives not employed by the company. |

| Date | CONFIDENTIAL | PAGE<br>5 of 6 |
|---|---|---|

| PROCEDURE MANUAL | Section<br>**PERSONNEL** |
|---|---|
| | Subject<br>**INTERVIEW GUIDELINES** |

| Subject | You MAY Ask* | You MAY NOT Ask* |
|---|---|---|
| Notify in Case of Emergency | Name and address of person to be notified in case of an accident or emergency. | |
| Military | Have you even been a member of the Armed Services or in a state militia? If so, did your military experience have any relationship to the position for which you have applied? | About an applicant's general military experience. |
| Organizations | Are you a member of any organization, etc. (exclude organizations, the name or character of which indicates race, creed, color; or national origin of members)? | List all clubs, societies, and lodges to which you belong. |
| References | Who suggested that you apply for a position here? | |

* Inquiries that would otherwise be deemed lawful may, in certain circumstances, be deemed as evidence of unlawful discrimination when the inquiry seeks to elicit information about a selection criterion which is not job-related and which has a disproportionately burdensome effect upon the members of a minority group and cannot be justified by business necessity.

| Date | CONFIDENTIAL | PAGE<br>6 of 6 |
|---|---|---|

## E. Record of Student Interview*

**RECORD OF STUDENT INTERVIEW**

*(Fill Out Immediately After Each Interview)*

Name:________________ College:________________

Degree:__________ Major__________ Date of Graduation:__________ 19____

**APPRAISAL OF CANDIDATE**

| TRAITS | EXCELLENT | GOOD | AVERAGE | BELOW AVERAGE | POOR |
|---|---|---|---|---|---|
| General First Impression | | | | | |
| Personal Appearance | | | | | |
| Apparent Drive | | | | | |
| Initiative in Conversation | | | | | |
| Apparent Aggressiveness | | | | | |
| Apparent Ability to Get Along with People | | | | | |
| Attitude | | | | | |
| Speech | | | | | |
| Potential | | | | | |
| Final Impression | | | | | |

**PERSONALITY** *(Check more than one)*

- Dominant ☐
- Strong ☐
- Passive ☐
- Negative ☐
- Quiet ☐
- Affable ☐
- Commonplace ☐
- Colorless ☐
- Excellent ☐
- Good ☐
- Pleasing ☐
- Poor ☐

**POISE AND MANNER**

- Overbearing ☐
- Confident ☐
- Ordinary ☐
- Awkward ☐
- Nervous ☐

**MATURITY (For Age)**

- Advanced ☐
- Normal ☐
- Immature ☐

**SUMMARY RATING**

| | SCHOLASTIC | EXTRA CURRICULAR | RELATED WORK EXPERIENCE | PERSONAL TRAITS | OVERALL |
|---|---|---|---|---|---|
| Outstanding | | | | | |
| Above Average | | | | | |
| Average | | | | | |
| Fair | | | | | |
| Not Qualified | | | | | |

**ADDITIONAL COMMENTS**

______________________________________________

______________________________________________

______________________________________________

______________________________________________

______________________________________________

______________________________________________

______________________________________________

RECOMMENDED FOR FURTHER INTERVIEW.................... Yes ☐ No ☐

RECOMMENDED FOR HIRE: THE COMPANY AS A WHOLE.......... Yes ☐ No ☐

YOUR PARTICULAR SECTION.......... Yes ☐ No ☐

DATE:________________ INTERVIEWED BY:________________

*Reprinted from *BNA Policy and Practice Series—Sample Policies and Forms* 5:309 (1993).

## F. Oral Interview Rating Form*

ORAL INTERVIEW RATING FORM ORAL DATE ______________

CANDIDATE'S NAME ______________________ POSITION INTERVIEWED FOR ______________

INSTRUCTIONS: You are to rate the candidate on his suitability for the position for which he [or she] is applying. To help you rate the candidates, five traits are suggested to assist you in arriving at a rating. The traits are not meant to be all inclusive, but are presented to assist you in determining a numerical rating. The statements under each trait are again an aid in determining a rating. Your final rating of the candidate will be shown on rating number 6 — SUITABILITY FOR THIS POSITION.

Please circle (70 1 2 3) the number on the scale where, in your opinion and judgment, the candidate stands.

1. APPEARANCE: Consider the candidate's personal appearance, bearing in mind the requirements of the position. Does the candidate give a satisfactory appearance as a representative of the local government?

Observe: dress, neatness, posture, sitting position, facial expressions, mannerisms.

| | | | | |
|---|---|---|---|---|
| 0 20 40 50 | 60 1 2 3 4 5 6 7 8 9 | 70 1 2 3 4 5 6 7 8 9 | 80 1 2 3 4 5 6 7 8 9 | 90 1 2 3 4 5 6 7 8 9 |
| Unacceptable | Unsatisfactory | Acceptable with reservation | Acceptable | Outstanding |

2. VOICE: Consider the quality of the candidate's voice in relation to the subject position. Does the candidate speak clearly and distinctly? Is his voice pleasant or harsh?

Observe: affected delivery, nasalized or muffled speech, loudness, softness, clearness, pleasantness.

| | | | | |
|---|---|---|---|---|
| 0 20 40 50 | 60 1 2 3 4 5 6 7 8 9 | 70 1 2 3 4 5 6 7 8 9 | 80 1 2 3 4 5 6 7 8 9 | 90 1 2 3 4 5 6 7 8 9 |
| Unacceptable | Unsatisfactory | Acceptable with reservation | Acceptable | Outstanding |

3. ABILITY TO USE THE ENGLISH LANGUAGE:
Consider the candidate's choice of words, sentences, phrases and use of slang.

Observe: use of simple and correct English, use of slang, hesitations, repeats needlessly technical word usage, logical presentation, coherence of thoughts.

| | | | | |
|---|---|---|---|---|
| 0 20 40 50 | 60 1 2 3 4 5 6 7 8 9 | 70 1 2 3 4 5 6 7 8 9 | 80 1 2 3 4 5 6 7 8 9 | 90 1 2 3 4 5 6 7 8 9 |
| Unacceptable | Unsatisfactory | Acceptable with reservation | Acceptable | Outstanding |

*Continued on next page*

*Reprinted from *BNA Policy and Practice Series—Sample Policies and Forms* 5:315 (1993).

4. SELF-CONFIDENCE:

Consider the candidate's self-control. Is the candidate nervous or ill at ease? Is he poised and relaxed? Does he appear to be uncertain or hesitant about himself or his ideas?

Observe: embarrassment, stammering, tension, poise, hesitation, confidence, timidness, over-confidence.

| 0 20 40 50 | 60 1 2 3 4 5 6 7 8 9 | 70 1 2 3 4 5 6 7 8 9 | 80 1 2 3 4 5 6 7 8 9 | 90 1 2 3 4 5 6 7 8 9 |
|---|---|---|---|---|
| Unacceptable | Unsatisfactory | Acceptable with reservation | Acceptable | Outstanding |

5. ABILITY TO GET ALONG WITH PEOPLE:

Consider the candidate's attitude toward the examiners. Does he appear to be friendly, polite. and likable? Does he command respect? Is he over-sensitive to criticism? Is there antagonism, indifference, a cooperative attitude?

| 0 20 40 50 | 60 1 2 3 4 5 6 7 8 9 | 70 1 2 3 4 5 6 7 8 9 | 80 1 2 3 4 5 6 7 8 9 | 90 1 2 3 4 5 6 7 8 9 |
|---|---|---|---|---|
| Unacceptable | Unsatisfactory | Acceptable with reservation | Acceptable | Outstanding |

6. SUITABILITY FOR THIS POSITION:

Consider whether the candidate will work out on the job. Does he reply readily to questions asked? Are his ideas original? Are statements convincing and appropriate? Is there evidence of leadership? Does he speak out voluntarily at proper times? Does he have a definite interest in this work?

Observe: alertness, responsiveness, tact, cooperation, enthusiasm.

| 0 20 40 50 | 60 1 2 3 4 5 6 7 8 9 | 70 1 2 3 4 5 6 7 8 9 | 80 1 2 3 4 5 6 7 8 9 | 90 1 2 3 4 5 6 7 8 9 |
|---|---|---|---|---|
| Unacceptable | Unsatisfactory | Acceptable with reservation | Acceptable | Outstanding |

7. GENERAL COMMENTS:

SIGNATURE OF RATER: ______________________

## G. Resume and Interview Evaluation*

**RESUME AND INTERVIEW EVALUATION**

Route to:

| Name of Applicant | Candidate for (Position Title) | Date |
|---|---|---|
| | | |

This form handles the application and interviewing phases of the employment process. PART A is to be completed after reviewing the resume and returned to Personnel. If a decision to interview is made, this form will be returned for the completion of PART B.

A. RESUME REVIEW — Attached is the resume of named applicant for your review. After review please complete the rest of PART A only.

☐ I AM INTERESTED

- ☐ Secure an application
- ☐ Invite for an interview
- ☐ Take no action now, but hold resume on file until Month ________ Year ________
- ☐ Obtain additional information listed below:

______________________________

______________________________

☐ I AM NOT INTERESTED

Reasons listed below:

______________________________

______________________________

B. Interview Evaluation Report — This section is to be completed only after the applicant has been interviewed. Please record the extent to which you feel the applicant possesses or will demonstrate the qualities listed below.

| | Out-standing | Above Average | Average | Below Average | Un-acceptable |
|---|---|---|---|---|---|
| 1. Aspirations — Extent to which the goals & aspirations of the applicant are consistent with available opportunities. | | | | | |
| 2. Training — Extent to which the applicant's level of educational attainment and relevant on-the-job training will enable him to cope with the demands of the job. | | | | | |
| 3. Work History — Extent to which the applicant's work experience can be applied in the performance of the duties involved in this position. | | | | | |
| 4. Manners & Appearance — Extent to which applicant is able to present & communicate his ideas to elicit favorable reactions from others. | | | | | |
| 5. Cooperation — Degree to which the applicant will be able to get along with others and work with them as a member of a team. | | | | | |
| 6. Poise — Degree to which the applicant will be able to maintain his composure under pressure and adjust to change in his work. | | | | | |
| 7. Responsibility — Extent to which the applicant will exercise judgment in getting the job done, taking the initiative where appropriate, and seeking assistance when required. | | | | | |

COMMENTS

______________________________

______________________________

| Disposition ☐ Offer ☐ No Interest ☐ Hold Until (Date): | Signed | Date |
|---|---|---|

---

*Reprinted from *BNA Policy and Practice Series—Sample Policies and Forms* 5:319 (1993).

## H. Employment of Relatives*

**EMPLOYMENT OF RELATIVES**

**(Western Hospital Association)**

Members of an employee's immediate family will be considered for employment on the basis of their qualifications. Immediate family may not be hired, however, if [employment] would:

- Create a supervisor/subordinate relationship with a family member;
- Have the potential for creating an adverse impact on work performance; or
- Create either an actual conflict of interest or the appearance of a conflict of interest.

This policy must also be considered when assigning, transferring, or promoting an employee. For the purposes of this policy, immediate family includes: mother, father, husband, wife, son, daughter, sister, brother, mother-in-law, father-in-law, sister-in-law, brother-in-law, son-in-law, daughter-in-law, and step-child. This policy also applies to close personal relationships.

Employees who marry or establish a close personal relationship may continue employment as long as it does not result in the above. If one of the conditions outlined should occur, attempts will be made to find a suitable position within [the Company] to which one of the employees will transfer. If accommodations of this nature are not feasible, the employees will be permitted to determine which of them will resign.

*Reprinted from *BNA Policy and Practice Series—Sample Policies and Forms* 5:51 (1993).

# IX. News Media and Photography

## A. News Media Relations*

<table>
<tr><td rowspan="3">Policy Title: NEWS MEDIA RELATIONS<br><br>Approved:</td><td colspan="2">Policy Number</td></tr>
<tr><td>Section</td><td>Page</td></tr>
<tr><td>M-22</td><td>1 of 1</td></tr>
<tr><td>- President<br>EMPLOYEE - V.P. -Human Resources<br>HANDBOOK & Public Relations</td><td colspan="2">Issue Date:<br><br>6-15-92</td></tr>
</table>

OBJECTIVE — To establish guidelines and define responsibilities for dealing with the news media.

POLICY — [Company Name] recognizes the value of a positive, cooperative working relationship with the news media. It is the policy of [Company Name] to cooperate with the news media by providing information for dissemination to the public to the extent that such information is not harmful to resources or assets of the Company, or does not create unreasonable risk for the Company or its assets.

AUTHORITY — All news media requests for information should be directed to the Public Relations Manager. The Public Relations Manager may use discretion to authorize other employees with specific expertise to respond to news media questions as appropriate.

In practice, department vice presidents are presumed to be authorized to address questions from the news media in their areas of expertise without advance authorization from the Public Relations Manager.

At certain times, it is appropriate for the Agriculture and Operations Managers, or their designees to respond directly to requests for information about local crop conditions or local factory operations. Such responses must be limited to the employee's area of expertise.

Other employees are explicitly <u>not</u> authorized to discuss the Company, its operations, businesses or products with representatives of the news media.

REPORT ALL REQUESTS — All news media contacts and inquiries are to be reported to the Public Relations Manager as soon as possible following the contact if such notification is impossible or impracticable before the contact.

RECORDS — A record should be kept of all contacts with news media representatives, and such contacts are to be reported to the Public Relations Manager. The record should include the name of the reporter, the news medium represented, the date and time of the contact, the nature of the information being requested, and the nature of any information provided by the employee.

RESPONSES — All requests from the news media should be addressed in a timely, courteous manner. If the Public Relations Manager is unavailable at the time of the request, news media requests should be forwarded to the appropriate department vice president.

---

*Reprinted from material received from members of BNA's Personnel Policies Forum.

## B. Photography on Company Premises*

| | | |
|---|---|---|
| **Policy Title:** PHOTOGRAPHY ON COMPANY PREMISES | Policy Number | |
| **Approved:** | Section | Page |
| | M-23 | 1 Of 1 |
| - President<br>**EMPLOYEE HANDBOOK** - V.P. -Human Resources & Public Relations | Issue Date:<br>6-15-92 | |

OBJECTIVE

To protect the assets of the Company by limiting the recording of visual information on Company premises to authorized Company personnel and approved visitors.

POLICY

Photography on Company premises is limited to those employees or visitors authorized by the President, department vice presidents, the Operations Managers, the Distribution Facilities Manager, or the Public Relations Manager.

For purposes of this policy, photography includes recording of visual information by any means whatsoever, including photographic film, video tape, and electronic disc.

REQUESTS TO PHOTOGRAPH

All requests to photograph Company facilities, equipment or processes which are considered confidential or proprietary should be referred to the ranking executive responsible for the facility in question, a corporate officer, or the Public Relations Manager to approve the requested photography.

To the extent possible, without compromising or risking corporate assets, photography will normally be allowed at Company facilities. However, the safety of visitors and employees must take priority over a person's desire to gain access to Company property or facilities for the purpose of photography. All employees are authorized and encouraged to report any photographic activity on Company premises which they feel may jeopardize the assets of the Company or put any visitor or employee at risk. Such reports should be made to security personnel, the ranking executive at the facility, a corporate officer, or the Public Relations Manager.

*Reprinted from material received from members of BNA's Personnel Policies Forum.

# Table of Cases

References are to chapter and footnote number (e.g., ***5***: 16 refers to footnote 16 in chapter 5).

**J**



**K**



**L**



**M**

## T



## V



## W



## Y



## Z